Anointed

Strategies

■ ■ ■

Power Plays

By Prince Handley

University of Excellence Press

ISBN-13: 978-0692814406
ISBN-10: 069281440X

UNIVERSITY OF EXCELLENCE PRESS
San Diego ◼ London ◼ Tel Aviv

Printed in the USA

First Edition

✚

The only Power Strategies book you need!

TABLE OF CONTENTS

FOREWORD

Whether you are an entrepreneur, a rabbi, a minister, a homemaker or a person who just became a follower of Messiah Jesus, you will—at times—need instruction.

Would you like a "how to do it" manual to consult so that you know what to do:

- When the BOTTOM falls out?

- AFTER your next success?

- If you are not SURE?

- To CREATE your future?

- If a person asks about EVOLUTION?

- When STRESS is attacking?

- About tension in RELATIONSHIPS

- A major secret for HEALTH?

There are several tricks, and diversionary tactics of the enemy to halt, hinder, impede, nullify or destroy your profession, your service for God, or your reputation.

This book will be your index of strategies ... and step-by-step instructions for absolute victory: spiritually, mentally, physically and materially.

5

You will be provided with precise instructions on how to have victory over any attacks—and the person or people behind them—that oppose you.

The purpose of this book is to present **power plays** for the people of God—*especially those involved in God's work*—to provide **specific strategies** for advancement, health, production and victory ... and to guarantee deliverance, protection and success.

This book is composed of various real-life scenarios that can face, buffet, attack, humiliate or disable a child of God. Such situations may be designed **and targeted** especially against those who labor in God's Vineyard. **It's already happening**.

What you are going to learn about are **real situations**, and HOW to—*not just cope with them*—but overcome them and come out on the other side victorious.

Then, you can go help others!

Anointed

Strategies

■ ■ ■

Power Plays

POWER PLAYS

You are reading this book while several seen and unseen—known and unknown—forces are being devised against God's People. What could be described as a "warm up" to the final games in the End Times.

The purpose of this book is to present **power plays** for the people of God—especially those involved in God's work—to provide **specific strategies** for advancement, health, production and victory ... and to guarantee deliverance, protection and success.

This book is composed of various real life scenarios that can face, buffet, attack, humiliate or disable a child of God. Such situations may be designed **and targeted** especially to those who labor in God's Vineyard. **It's already happening**. What you are going to learn about are real situations, and HOW to—not just cope with them—but overcome them and come out on the other side victorious. How you do so will determine your destiny—and the destiny of multitudes—in this life ... and forever.

As for the **POWER PLAYS**, you will learn about:

■ Why some situations arise.

■ The players behind the scenes.

■ The importance of discernment.

■ What to do after the victory.

Then ... you can go help other people be victorious!

GROWING FORESTS – HOW TO GROW WHAT YOU WANT

This first chapter will teach you HOW to grow forests through your thinking, your ideas, and even your attitudes! It works IF you know the SECRET.

Learn to ACT towards God at the point of decision.

Your inner thought processes are constantly planting NEW FORESTS that will either grow to your advantage or disadvantage. But you need to know MORE than this.

This section contains a SECRET that was revealed to me by a man of God before he died ... AND ... it was revealed to him by a man of God before he died.

Get ready for your life, your productivity, your success ... and your whole future to change: for the BETTER!

Pray ahead of time for wisdom to know HOW to handle this GREAT harvest of **growing what you want!**

If your plans fit into God's plans ...

You will have God's faith ...

And, God's faith always works!

While at a large metropolitan city—I don't remember where—I was in a hotel room reflecting, praying, and meditating before going to minister. Several stories up, I was looking out over the city to a large forest. I thought, *"Where did all those trees come from?"* As quickly as I had this thought, came an answer: *"From a seed."*

What kind of forest would you like—or need—to grow today? Is it a forest for your family, for your ministry, for the nations of the world . . . or for something personal in your life? Most of you reading this teaching already know about sowing and reaping. That is not the purpose of this teaching. **What I want to teach you in this section is:** *How to grow forests through your thinking, your ideas, and even your attitudes!*

King David was a prime example of growing forests: he thought "God thoughts." He had an idea of how to use his sling shot to penetrate a small opening in the armor of Goliath, and he had a positive attitude versus a nine foot giant. He knew intimately his God and trusted Him.

However, **King David grew forests both positive and negative**. In the positive sense, he drew from his experience and skill as a shepherd, and killed Goliath; which act later catapulted David into the office of King and leader over Israel. In the negative sense, he lusted after Bathsheba, which act played itself out in adultery with her and the murder of her husband, Uriah.

The result was fourfold judgment on David's own household:

> 1. The death of David's child who was born by Bathsheba (Uriah's wife).

> 2. The rape of Tamar, David's 15 year old virgin daughter, by his 22 year old son Amnon.

> 3. The murder of Amnon by Absalom, Amnon's younger brother.

> 4. Absalom's treason against King David, his father, resulting in Absalom's death.

These four (4) judgments were actually the fulfillment of a prophecy (a message from God) which Nathan, the prophet, delivered to King David because of David's crime of adultery with Bathsheba, Uriah's wife, and the subsequent murder of Uriah. This prophecy, which Nathan related to David as a story about a rich man with many sheep who stole his poor neighbor's only lamb, **was actually according to the demands of the Law** (to restore fourfold any sheep stolen) **in Torah: Exodus 22:1**.

This is where the POINT OF DECISION is so important. **Learn to ACT towards God at the point of decision.** My mother used to say, *"You should have nipped it in the bud."* We are continuously growing forests: either negatively or positively. This is why Jesus said: *"For a* beautiful tree does not produce worthless fruit; neither does a rotten tree produce valuable fruit." (Luke 6:43)

We are not just planting forests when we give money. We are continuously growing forests—*positive forests or negative forests*—good forests or bad forests! *"Be not deceived; God is not mocked: for whatsoever a man sows, he shall also reap the same."* (Galatians 6:7)

Jesus also instructed us:

"For from within, out of the heart of men, proceed evil thoughts, adulteries, fornications, murders, thefts, covetousness, wickedness, deceit, lasciviousness, an evil eye, blasphemy, pride, foolishness: all these things come from within, and defile the man." (Mark 7:21-23) This is why the Proverbs admonish us, *"For as a person thinks in his heart, so is he."* (Proverb 23:7)

In Job 22:28 we read, *"You shall also decree a thing, and it shall be established unto you ..."* In the original Hebrew language the word "decree" is a primitive root form of the word "gazar", which means **"to cut out exclusively, or to decide."** In its primitive form it is used also as a "quarrying" term ... as in cutting out stone from a rock quarry. It means more than to "say" or "speak". **It conveys the meaning of "cutting something out in your mind's eye;"** that is, "to envision [to make a vision], **to decide upon it**, and confess it" ... and then it will be established unto you!

12

Learn to control your heart, your inner thought processes! **Your inner thought processes are constantly planting NEW FORESTS that will either grow to your advantage or disadvantage.** This is one reason the Bible says in 1 Corinthians 13 that *"Love . . . believes all things, hopes all things."* (Verse 7) **Faith works through love.** (Galatians 5:6)

So we first must have a vehicle (or, a conduit) through which our faith can work. I have heard people spouting words of faith who at the same time didn't seem to be emanating much love. We, at times—*especially in difficult situations*—have to back up one step and ASK God for love. Then, we can believe all things, hope all things. **Then, we can grow large quality forests.**

How many times have you had a thought that played out? Maybe it was something good that you really wanted—or maybe it was something you were afraid of. I was talking to a person on the phone recently who was not a believer and who said to me, *"Whenever I have a thought about something it happens to me."*

Learn to spend quality time meditating and thinking—visualizing in the mind's eye of your heart—the GREAT THINGS you want to do for God. Plant and grow GIANT FORESTS of good. Remember, God promised you that He is *"able to do exceeding abundantly above all that you ask or think."* (Ephesians 3:20)

Spend time planting and cultivating your forest. Any worthwhile thing in life takes time, so why not spend good quality time planning and preparing your forest. Invest in yourself … and in your future!

My friend, remember this -

> *If your plans fit into God's plans ...*
> *You will have God's faith ...*
> *And, God's faith always works!*

Find out God's Plans by reading and studying His Holy Word: His plans for YOU, for your relationships, for your work and for Israel.

PREVENTING BAD FORESTS – REVELATION AND DECISION

This chapter will teach you HOW to prevent BAD forests from growing and advancing in your life.

The point of decision is the juncture leading into two opposite paths and **resulting in either growth—or—diminishing returns.** It is the "gateway" to either good forests—or—bad forests. Make sure you are growing continued success. Protect yourself from degradation of anointed production.

People have a **false** sense of peace when the enemy stops bothering them. They are NOT any longer experiencing his agitation and temptations to a greater degree than previously.

Creativity and NEW ideas will sustain your anointing if you follow the SECRET in this book.

However, there is a REAL sense of peace that accompanies obedience, productivity and anointing. In this environment you experience creativity and powerful ideas that provide growth of spiritual and material substance.

When you have a good idea, other things many times interrupt you. Why do you think this happens? The material in this section is written to provide you with Spirit anointed revelation for your protection—and to protect you from growing bad forests.

In the previous section we discussed *Growing Forests* and briefly discussed the importance of the POINT OF DECISION. In this section we will discuss the contradistinction of growing GOOD forests, and teach you **how to prevent bad forests**: forests that wreck lives, families, and ministries. Preparation ahead of time is invaluable because your enemy is already—and always—planning for your demise. In this teaching I am going to provide you with **revealed knowledge** upon which you may act ... and thereby enable you to successfully resist the devil and prevent bad forests from growing.

First of all, let me say that the Word of God teaches us to *"Resist the devil, and he will flee from you."* (James 4:7) However—in the forerunner of the last days in which we live—the enemy has **many tricks with which both to allure and to deceive you in an attempt to position you in a state of spiritual lethargy**. The reason for this strategy is so that you will be caught in his (the devil's) trap and not want to resist—until it's too late.

He may attack you unwittingly at first in a dream, through an advertisement, in a medium of entertainment ... or in thought. He knows that you know the Word of God. The enemy has to work through BOTH your mind and your senses.

In the previous chapter we discussed growing GOOD forests through your thinking, your ideas, and even your attitudes. We also discussed that you can grow BAD forests. This is where the **POINT OF DECISION** is so important. If you haven't already, read Chapter One again: *Growing Forests: How to Grow What You Want*. It is extremely important!

When you have a good idea, other things many times interrupt you. Why do you think this happens? Usually, it is none other than the work of Satan. Let me explain—*through revealed knowledge given to me by the Holy Spirit*—how the enemy works upon you. The devil is like a man who takes advantage of a woman, and then leaves her. He takes advantage of you by tempting you with an idea. You SEE the idea. Your carnal man then wants, or desires, to be involved in the action, or implementation, of the idea.

After the activity is initiated and then consummated, the following things happen:

> The anointing of the Holy Spirit leaves you;
>
> The devil leaves you;***
>
> False peace enters; and then,
>
> Conviction enters (an awareness that something is wrong).

***Notice: The devil will not leave you (that is, stop badgering you) until the anointing leaves you. That's why people then have a false sense of peace. They are NOT any longer experiencing the agitation and temptation of the enemy. (He doesn't need to bother them at this juncture, because **he finished his job: to get them to lose the anointing**.)

This doesn't mean they don't have the Holy Spirit in them, or that they can't win souls, witness, or minister—it means that they have ceased being a "new sharp threshing instrument" in Kingdom work—**the anointing is gone**. Samson didn't have the Holy Spirit IN him, but he had the anointing of the Spirit upon him for service until he lost it. King David cried out, after he had sinned, *"Take not your Holy Spirit from me."*

This is why the POINT OF DECISION is so important. As soon as you have a BAD IDEA, do the following:

1. Resist the devil with the Word of God. (James 4:7)

2. If the drawing of Satan (the temptation) is too strong, you MUST take the "way of escape" immediately. This is because the enemy has already gained a foothold in your mind and or senses.

> *"There has no temptation taken you but such as is common to man, but God is faithful, who will not sallow you to be tempted above that which you are able (to withstand); but will with the temptation*

18

also make a way of escape, that you may be able to bear it." – 1 Corinthians 10:13

You MUST **want** to take the "way of escape." My job in this teaching is to reveal to you, by the help of the Holy Spirit, **how much Satan hates you**. He wants to ruin your life, your family and your ministry. **The devil does NOT want you to be the powerful instrument God has made of you.** You need to SEE THIS FACT. You can give the devil NO PLACE from which he may operate or attack you. The enemy is really trying to attack God and His Kingdom through you.

This is why—if you will read the context of the passage in Corinthians—the Spirit says in the previous verse: *"Wherefore let him that thinks he stand take heed lest he fall."* (Verse 12)

The temptation may be to do anything contrary to the will of God. (The Word of God is the WILL of God.) The temptation may be in any form. The enemy knows where you are most vulnerable; once you have learned to protect yourself in these areas, he will try to devise NEW MEANS to attack you: new ideas to allure you.

3. Immediately, get on your knees and cry out to God to deliver you. Scripture tells us, *"And call upon me in the day of trouble: I will deliver you, and you shall glorify me."* (Psalm 50:15)

The POINT OF DECISION is where you have to act ... **you have to move toward God**. The enemy is called "the serpent" because he is slithery and deadly. Many Christians—some of them leaders, anointed by God—have lost the anointing and grown bad forests. **They thought they could stand, and let down their guard**.

You and I are in a war which comprises **many** continuous spiritual battles. **Our Commander-in-Chief has promised us victory if we listen to His directives**. My purpose in this teaching is to remind you of how vicious the enemy is, and how he will try to subtly attack you just like he did Eve in the garden. The enemy will use three (3) areas of attack:

- The lust of the flesh—**appetite**—the taste (good for food).

- The lust of the eyes—**appeal**—good to look upon.

- The pride of life—**applause**—the desire to make one wise.

The Apostle John wrote: *"Love not the world, neither the things that are in the world. If any person loves the world, the love of the Father is not in him. For all that is in the world—the lust of the **flesh**, the lust of the **eyes**, and the **pride** of life—is not of the Father, but is of the world. And* *the world passes away, and the lust thereof; but he that does the will of God abides forever."* (1 John 2:15-17)

Commit your works to the LORD and your thoughts will be established. (Proverbs 16:3) The Master has need of you. Do NOT let somebody be hurt—and do NOT let your Savior be hurt—as a result of you growing BAD forests.

The POINT OF DECISION is where you have to act. Grow GOOD forests: for your family, your ministry, for the nations of the world … and for yourself!

THAT'S WHAT FRIENDS ARE FOR

You need to be continually in the **peace zone**. In this chapter I will share with you two (2) important areas where the enemy of your soul wants to attack you in order to keep you out of the peace zone. They are:

■ Making bad or unwise decisions; and,

■ Maintaining unresolved conflicts.

This section will cover both areas for you. Plus—in this chapter **you will learn how to enjoy victory over your enemies**. God can turn the situation around and use them to develop you, while bringing you into new areas of usefulness and productivity!

You will learn about a spiritual security system—a burglar alarm—that will protect you. **In some cases you will be dealing with a person who is temporarily mentally "off center."** You need to know HOW to respond in these types of situations.

Of utmost importance is a SECRET you will learn to help you stay in the peace zone.

In Chapter One we discussed *Growing Forests* and briefly discussed the importance of the POINT OF DECISION. In Chapter Two we discussed *Preventing Bad Forests*: forests that wreck lives, families, and ministries. Preparation ahead of time is invaluable because your enemy is already, and always, planning for your demise.

In this book chapter I am going to provide you with revealed knowledge upon which you may act. Specifically, I will discuss aggravation and offense—and HOW God can use your enemies to promote you.

> *"Give none offence, neither to the Jews, nor to the Gentiles, nor to the church of God."* – 1 Corinthians 10:32

> *"Do not be overcome by evil, but overcome evil with good."* – Romans 12:21

A few years ago there was a popular song titled, *That's What Friends Are For*, and my favorite version was sung by Dionne Warwick, Stevie Wonder, Whitney Houston and Luther Vandross.

The KEY thing—*horizontally*—in your relationships with other people is this: **Don't offend people**. It's O.K. to offend the devil and demons. As a matter of fact ... it is fun! A good friend of mine, a commodities broker, used to tell me, *"If you want to cuss the devil, just pray in tongues."* What he meant is that praying in tongues hurts Satan and demons ... it drives them "crazier."

Many times people AND situations are "stirred up" by the devil to aggravate you and to get you out of—*or, to keep you out of*— the peace zone.

No matter what people do to you ... **stay in the peace zone**.

___

Stay in the PEACE zone!

___

If you need a friend, I am here to help YOU. That's my assignment from God

> *Keep smiling!*
>
> *Keep shining!*
>
> *Knowing you can always count on God.*
>
> *That's what friends are for ... in good times ... in bad times.*
>
> *Jesus will be on your side forevermore ... for that's what friends are for.*

Sometimes people close to you may offend you ... **they may be Christians or relatives or friends**. But your job is to NOT offend. **Stay in the peace zone**. Another way you can stay in the peace zone is by **NOT making bad decisions ...** or even, "hasty" decisions: things you are NOT sure about. I have written a book to help you in that area titled, *Decision Making 101 – Know for Sure*

Learn to ENJOY VICTORY over your enemies—God can use them to develop you and thrust you into new areas of usefulness and productivity. Joseph, Daniel, Mordecai and Esther are all prime examples of how God can use your enemies to advance you, and to bring both DELIVERANCE and ENLARGEMENT for you and others. Use your faith—utilize the love and the forgiveness of God—and **leave the TIME up to God!**

You don't have to FEEL like loving them—just **know** that God wants you to love them, and then make a conscious decision to do it. Ask God to give you love, forgiveness and WISDOM in dealing with them. SEE them as someone whom God:

> 1. Has put in your path for you to share the testimony of God.
>
> 2. Has placed before you to draw out His resources: His love, provision and gifts.
>
> 3. Has prepared to enable your spiritual growth.
>
> 4. Has chosen to use for your advancement and promotion.

Then, knowing the above—**when you see the attacks coming**—rejoice and praise God! Then take your authority over Satan, and bind him in Jesus' name from carrying out his insidious attacks. Many times the person or people opposing you will be working unwittingly with another person to attack you. Why? Because they hate you and they are jealous of the Christ that is in you.

If you are a married person, and the attack is coming from your Christian spouse, then learn to **get alone and worship the Christ that is in them!** Watch what happens!

Many times you may be lied about. The person telling the lies may be a psychopathic or pathological liar. **This may be a case involving a spouse or close business associate.** If so, then—as my mother many times said—*"You made your bed, so you'll have to sleep in it!"* In that case, you must **deal with the strategies of Satan through the gift of discernment**.

If a person is just telling lies about you because of jealousy, envy, hatred—or because the enemy is stirring them to attack you for some reason—then you can learn to see them as someone God has positioned for any of numbers 1, 2, 3, and 4 above. Again, **learn to ENJOY VICTORY over your enemies—God can turn the situation around and use them to develop you, while bringing you into new areas of usefulness and productivity!**

Actually, as a shepherd and warrior, you should begin to use these opportunities to put Satan to flight. *"Submit yourselves therefore to God. Resist the devil, and he will flee from you."* [James 4:7]

What you want to do is learn to develop your spiritual "burglar alarm." You need a spiritual security system! **Ask God for the gift of discernment**. This way you will know when the attacks are active and you can begin to enjoy taking opportunity of them in the Spirit. Pray in the Spirit—in tongues.

Warning: this will usually make the person or people more angry and jealous; however, God will use this to bring extra conviction upon them to accomplish His purpose(s).

In some cases you will be dealing with a person who is temporarily mentally "off center." They may have a lot of pressure upon them; they may have old hurts that somehow they associate with you; or they may be just oppressed by the enemy and he is using them as an instrument to attack you.

This is where you have to be really on guard! **Just because a person is mentally incapacitated does NOT mean they're stupid**. Let me use an example by means of a story. A man was driving down the road and one of his tires became flat. It so happened that when he came to a stop where he could change the flat he was parked **on top of a ridge next to a mental hospital**.

While changing the tire, a patient of the mental hospital was watching him through the other side of the chain fence. The driver of the car was putting all the lug nuts from the wheel into the hub cap as he removed them. By accident, he stepped on the hub cap and all the lug nuts fell down the ridge ... they were lost. He was in despair and didn't know what to do!

The mental patient yelled across to him and said, *"Why don't you take one lug nut off each of the other three wheels and then use them on the tire you're changing."* *"That's a wonderful idea,"* said the driver. Then the driver said to the mental patient, *"I thought you were crazy?!"* *"I am,"* said the patient, *"but that doesn't mean I'm stupid!"*

Many times, and at different intervals, God will call you to shepherd KEY enemies. David shepherded Goliath and later Saul. Moses shepherded Pharaoh. **The secret here is to remember that a good shepherd is also a good warrior.** He protects the flock and he also drives off the enemy.

You may be in a work situation at your business or place of employment where the things described above are happening to you. Learn to enjoy watching God work! Above all, **do NOT EMBRACE THE SPIRIT(S) of the person/people trying to aggravate you.** If you argue, or embrace the spirit working through them, then you will be in the flesh, and you have lost the battle. **Don't let YOUR spirit be aggravated!**

"He who has knowledge spares his words, and a man of understanding is of a calm (or, cool) spirit. Even a fool is counted wise when he holds his peace; when he shuts

his lips, he is considered perceptive." [Proverbs 17:27-28]

I trust this will help you. God has given you everything you need to **stay in the peace zone**. Just rely on Him. Don't worry about what you will do if a certain situation arrives. **When you need it, the wisdom and power will be there!**

And, if you happen (now or in the future) to find yourself in a situation with others that needs healing, check out my book titled, *Conflict Healing – Relational Health*.

THAT'S WHAT PROPHETS ARE FOR

You need to continually be in the blessing zone.

In this chapter you will learn two (2) important areas where members of the Body of Messiah—possibly including YOU—are being cheated out of blessing. These two areas are:

- Not listening for the call to be a Prophet; and,

- Not recognizing and honoring a Prophet.

This section will cover both areas ... Plus TWO (2) prophecies. Also, several real life incidents will be described where people did NOT honor the office of the Prophet.

You will learn the different functions of a prophet —PLUS—**a revelation of a unique End Time job description of the office of certain prophets**.

Also covered will be information dealing with the history and the importance of women prophets (including young girls).

Hang on! You're about to be transported into **a new dimension**—*but in addition*—receive **a new mantle!**

One of the greatest areas of ministry that is still being overlooked—*and under sought after*—is the office of Prophet.

In Chapter One we discussed *Growing Forests* and briefly discussed the importance of the POINT OF DECISION. In Chapter Two we discussed the contradistinction of growing GOOD forests versus bad forests, and **how to prevent bad forests**: forests that wreck lives, families, and ministries. Preparation ahead of time is invaluable because your enemy is already, and always, planning for your demise.

In Chapter Three we provided you with revealed knowledge upon which you may act in situations dealing with aggravation and offense—and HOW God can use your enemies to promote you. In this chapter, one of our goals is to share with you two important areas where members of the Body of Messiah—*possibly including YOU*—are being cheated out of blessing.

▓ Not listening for the call to be a Prophet; and,

▓ Not recognizing and honoring a Prophet.

31

In this teaching we will cover both areas ... plus two prophecies.

You need to continually be in the blessing zone.

"Now therefore restore the man his wife; for he is a prophet, and he shall pray for you, and you shalt live: and if you restore her not, you can know that you shall surely die, you, and all that are yours."

— Genesis 20:7

"He that receives a prophet in the name of a prophet will receive a prophet's reward."

— Yeshua (Jesus) / Matthew 10:41

"He let no man do them wrong: Yes, he reproved leaders of nations for their sakes, saying, 'Touch not mine anointed, and do my prophets no harm.'"

— Psalm 105:15

In my book, *Conflict Healing,* I describe several incidents where people had opposed me in my ministry and what happened to them as a result:

- One lady drove her brand new yellow Cadillac through the back wall of her garage and into the swimming pool—she could have drowned, but for God's mercy—and was on the front page of three large newspapers:

  Los Angeles Times;

  Long Beach Press Telegram; and,

  Orange County (Santa Ana) Register.

- One young man died of a brain hemorrhage in 24 hours.

- One lady's house was destroyed to the ground in 48 hours.

These are just a few, plus several I did NOT include in the book.

Remember when Elijah withstood and challenged the false prophets on Mt. Carmel, and called fire down from Heaven (1 Kings 18). I was laughing the other day remembering when I was holding a tent meeting in Tennessee (USA). We had to cut down tall trees from the woods and drag them in by tractor to make poles to hold up the tent. One morning I was in the woods by myself praying for that night's meeting and asking God to **answer by fire from Heaven**.

I was kneeling in the woods on a tree stump suddenly I heard noises. I looked around and on every side of me there were BIG black bulls. Immediately I thought of the scripture in Psalm 22:11-12, *"Be not far from me; for trouble is near; for there is none to help. Many bulls have compassed me: strong bulls of Bashan have beset me round."* I don't know if I have ever prayed harder in my life! I prayed and prayed and prayed—and stayed and stayed and stayed—until finally the bulls moved away out of sight. Talk about being delivered!

Well, that night I preached on Elijah confronting the false prophets and **calling down fire from Heaven**. God had really been blessing the meetings and college students were driving from 70 miles away to come to the meetings. When I ended the meeting that night, I prayed, ***"Hear me, O LORD God, and let fire come down from Heaven."*** All of a sudden, smoke began to enter the tent from above!!! One of the large lights at the top of the wooden pole near the front where I was preaching overheated and **started burning the wooden pole** ... and **people ran to the altar**. One college student fell on the ground—under the power of the Holy Spirit—and remained there under the power of God. At that time in my life I was NOT baptized in the Holy Spirit and I did not know what was happening to the young man.

34

Several college students gave their lives to be missionaries for the LORD God that night. And one of the students was later raised up to be a pastor in that area. **It does NOT matter HOW God works ... just so He works.**

Elijah was a man—a human being—just like we are. Yet, he prayed and God stopped the rain for three years. He prayed again, and God brought rain back on the earth again. **Elijah was NOT afraid to confront the leader of the nation.** Where are the REAL prophets today? **Sin is rampant because the office of the Prophet is being neglected: being vacated.**

One of the greatest areas of ministry that is still being overlooked—*and under sought after*—is the office of Prophet. I want to share with you two (2) important areas where the enemy wants to cheat the Body of Messiah—to rob the synagogue and church—out of blessing. These attacks from the enemy are designed to deceive God's People so that they will:

▪ NOT listen to the call to be a Prophet; or,

▪ NOT recognize and honor the office of the Prophet.

Of course, NOT all of God's People are called to the office of Prophet. However, the sad thing is—due to bad, inaccurate teaching from teachers and seminaries—most people do NOT know there is such an office. I am

NOT talking here about the Gift of Prophecy ... I am talking about the **office** of the Prophet.

God uses prophets for different reasons and for different prophetic discourses. Prophecy can be:

- Directed (to a particular person or group)

- Specific (as to present or future action or resulting from past action)

- National (pertaining to a country or ethnic amalgamation)

- Judgmental (resulting from transgression of God's principles)

- Contradictory (against false prophecies being declared)

- Notification of blessing (due to God's favor or the result of obedience)

To the above mentioned I want to ADD a category that is often overlooked by rabbis, ministers and theologians: **Prophecy can be used by God through the Prophet as a "Spotter."** Let me give you an example. If you follow NASCAR racing you may be familiar with the term "Spotter." **A high speed professional auto racer definitely needs a Spotter**: a person who is also **an experienced driver but who is an observer of the race in a special location above** the crowd who can see the cars, the line up of drivers, the track condition and opportunities for the driver to go ahead and pass, as well as pitfalls for the driver to avoid. **Many times the ministry of the Prophet is used in similar—parallel— life circumstances: to direct and guide people or nations through troubled waters.**

The prophetic spotter will be much needed in the future with genome alteration, human enhancement, brain-machine interfacing and cyber intelligence. *"Surely the Lord GOD will do nothing, but he reveals His secret unto his servants the prophets."*– Amos 3:7

You need to be continually in the blessing zone. One prerequisite for this is that **you need to be always listening to God ... and be open to what He is saying.** God does NOT change. And, the office of the Prophet has NOT changed. If you are NOT listening and someone calls you for dinner, you will probably miss dinner. **Are YOU listening to determine IF God is calling YOU to the office of Prophet?** And, I am NOT just talking to men. I am addressing this question to women—and girls—as well. **Women have been used since time past in the office of Prophet ... as well as men.**

Huldah was a Prophet. **Huldah is one of the seven women prophets of Israel enumerated by the Rabbis: Sarah, Miriam, Deborah, Hannah, Abigail, Huldah and Esther** (BT Megillah 14a). She is also mentioned among the twenty-three truly upright and righteous women who came forth from Israel (Midrash *Tadshe*, *Ozar ha-Midrashim* [Eisenstein], p. 474).

When King Josiah found the Torah scroll in the House of the Lord, he sent messengers to the prophet Huldah—and not to Jeremiah—probably hoping that she would be merciful in her prophecy (BT *Megillah* 14b). Josiah apparently hoped that Huldah would be more moderate in her revelations, or that her compassion would succeed in canceling the anticipated future tribulations. However, contrary to his expectations, **Huldah uttered harsh prophecies to the king.**

The greatest meetings where I have been on stage to observe closely as a minister were at the meetings of Kathryn Kulhman. Miss Kuhlman used to say often, *"If God would have found a man to do this job, he would NOT have chosen me."* I say that to emphasize—**and to prophesy**—that **God is getting ready to raise up and call out women as Prophets in these last days**: holy women filled with the Ruach HaChodesh (the Holy Spirit), filled with His Word, and who operate in the Gifts of the Spirit—**women who are NOT afraid to confront the leaders of nations**, openly or otherwise!

As when God calls men, so it is when He calls women. Your background is NOT the reason for your calling. **Who you are** does NOT depend on what you have or do not have, what education you have or do not have, what you do or do not do, who you know or do not know, or what you have done or have not done. **God calls**

YOU because of WHAT you will do and WHO is in you.

Huldah answered the messengers from King Josiah when they came to hear the Word of the LORD from her: *"Tell the man who sent you to me."* (2 Kings 22:15) Ancient Rabbis comment that because of her haughty deportment, she was given a derogatory name, "*huldah*," meaning "weasel" (BT *Megillah* 14b). However, I believe that Huldah may have possibly been—previously a "sneaky, untrustworthy, or insincere person" until the God of Israel changed her and called her to be a Prophet. (Just like He changed Jacob, Moses and, just like He has changed—or, will change—many people reading this, including me.)

In Psalm 68:11, we read: *"The Lord gave the word: great was the company of those that published it."* The literal translation of *"Great was the company [feminen gender] of those that published it"* is: *"Of the female preachers there was a great host."*

God has always used women. **God does NOT change—neither has the office of Prophet changed.** *"And the next day we that were of Paul's company departed, and came unto Caesarea: and we entered into the house of Philip the evangelist, which was one of the seven; and abode with him. And **the same man had four daughters, virgins, which did prophesy**."* – Acts 21:8-9

Several decades ago I prophesied that God was going to start raising up African Americans—and other Black People—for leadership in government, business and ministry and placing them in strategic positions. Now, **I prophesy to you that God is going to raise up KEY women He has chosen for the office of Prophet.**

The fringe benefits that go with the office of Prophet are wonderful. *"He let no man do them wrong: Yes, he reproved leaders of nations for their sakes, saying, 'Touch not mine anointed, and do my prophets no harm.'"* – Psalm 105:15

Now, let me give you a second prophecy. I want to quote from Ecclesiastes 3:1. *"To every thing there is a season, and a time to every purpose under the heaven."* My friend, **you are beginning to enter a NEW season. Your life is NOT over ... it is just beginning ... if you will receive this word and believe this prophecy.** You are entering a NEW season, my friend. Listen to God, obey God, be used by God ... and be BLESSED by God.

I trust this teaching will help you. God has given you everything you need to **stay in the blessing zone.** Check to see if you are:

- Listening to God's call to be a Prophet; and,

- Recognizing and honoring the office of the Prophet.

40

And, if you need help making a decision—or if you feel that you have NOT recognized and honored the office of a particular Prophet—check out the following books titled, *Decision Making 101 ... Conflict Healing – Relational Health ...* ***PLUS*** *... How to Receive God's Power with Gifts of the Spirit,* which will enable you to receive God's Power with resultant gifts.

LET IT GO AND FORGET ABOUT IT

You need to continually be in the freedom zone.

In this chapter you will learn about nine (9) unholy demon "loans." They are "loans" because they are the **opposite** of Holy Spirit "gifts."

If you embrace these unholy "loans" you will be locked to them just as "the borrower is servant to the lender."

The purpose of this section is to **provide you with a SECRET FORMULA for removing aggravating resistance and opposition against you, your family, your profession and your finances.**

You will be provided with precise instructions on how to have victory over any attacks—and the person or people behind them—that oppose you. Then you can help others, also!

Do NOT embrace that spirit.

Let it go ... forget about it.

In the last few weeks I have been involved in counseling people—*from different countries, but with the same problems*—who came to me for help concerning the same situation. These people were all Spirit-filled Christians and all but one were not only active in ministry, but powerful in ministry.

My advice in a "nutshell" for each of them was **"Let it go! Forget about it!"** Amazingly enough, after telling each of them the same thing, one night I had a little time to watch Christian TV. I happened to turn to a Christian program where Pastor Joel Osteen of Lakewood Church in Houston, Texas (USA) was teaching on the subject: *"Let it go!"*

Pastor Osteen's father used to listen to my teaching on cassette tapes and one time when I was in Houston at his church, Pastor John Osteen said (about me) *"This man's teachings are good!"* That was a real encouragement to me as a young minister.

My take on "LET IT GO" is a bit different than what Joel Osteen was teaching on, although his was excellent. My revelation is that as long as you HOLD to an issue where people are opposing you, you are "tied" to the situation. It is a **spiritual** tie ... and can end up subjecting a person to bondage.

Let me give you an example. Let's suppose you are working efficiently and productively at your place of employment and you have made your employer lots of money. One of your supervisors recommended you for a raise in pay and a promotion. However, both were denied by someone unknown. After that, you were promised twice that you would get the raise in pay and that it would be retroactive (payments made up) back to the time of your previous supervisor's recommendation. However, again you were told "No!" Well, after inquiring over and over about the matter you could be embittered, or quit your job, or mad at whoever was opposing your pay raise and job promotion. **This is an example of HOW demons work at you—opposing you and aggravating you—from "behind the scenes."**

When you embrace those—hidden, unknown—spirits you are "tied" to them. They have you bound to that "spiritual" setting, or environment. **Let it go! Break loose!** Follow the instructions I am about to give you and you will have victory and complete freedom in such situations.

SCENARIO: After praying and taking spiritual authority over both the situation and the people involved (even if unknown), let's suppose that you decide NOT to embrace that spirit of opposition—and to **cut yourself loose from it emotionally, physically and spiritually**—and turn the situation over into the hands of God. You will immediately experience peace: **you will be in the peace zone!**

Do NOT embrace the spirit of opposition; otherwise you

will end up being in a spiritual "lock." **Just let it go ... forget about it.**

There are three (3) KEY steps to obtaining victory in such situations:

- Authority;

- Release; and

- Transfer.

AUTHORITY

You must first take your (spiritual) authority over the situation. Bind the people, or demon spirits, or causative elements of opposition: those people and/or things that are troubling you or your ministry. Bind them in Jesus' name and cast them out from hindering you. Lock them up in the name of Jesus from opposing you or causing dissension.

RELEASE

I believe there are at least nine (9) unholy spirit (demon) loans. **These are "loans" because they are the opposite of Holy Spirit "gifts."** Once you accept a demonic "loan" you are bound to it: you owe it as long as you embrace it. Remember, the Holy Bible tells us, *"The borrower is servant to the lender."* (Proverb 22:7)

You may ask the question: *"How does one embrace an*

unholy spirit?" ANSWER: By accepting its invitation. **If it is a spirit of argumentativeness, you argue with it; thereby accepting its invitation.** You become entwined with it; you are entangled with it. You are embracing that evil spirit. The definition of "embrace" is:

- To take or clasp in the arms; press to the bosom; hug.

- To take or receive gladly or eagerly; accept willingly: to embrace an idea.

- To avail oneself of: to embrace an opportunity.

- To adopt (a profession or a religion, etc.).

- To take in with the eye or the mind.

Here are some **examples of unholy demon loans** (there may be more) as follows:

- Remembrance

- Argumentativeness

- Struggle

- Contention

- Competition

- Opposition

46

- Discord

- Negativity

- Condescension

For example, if you embrace the spirit of opposition, then you are locked to it: it has you "tied" to it. **Just release it ... AND ... the people or things promoting or causing it.** By "release" I mean **not just the act of forgiving**, but **"completely divorcing yourself from the situation."**

TRANSFER

After you have taken your spiritual authority over the people, spirits and elements that have been troubling, perplexing or opposing you, then transfer the situation into God's hands. In the Brit Chadashah (the New Testament), Rabbi Shaul (the Apostle Paul) admonishes us as follows:

*"Be anxious for nothing, but in everything by prayer and supplication **with thanksgiving**, let your requests be known to God; and the peace of God, which surpasses all understanding, will guard your hearts and minds through Messiah Jesus."* (Philippians 4:6)

The **KEY** is to transfer your situation to God **with thanksgiving**. This lets God know you are doing this in faith ... **you are already thanking Him for handling the situation and taking care of it for you.**

The original Greek term for the English "will guard your hearts and minds" is **military terminology** and means **"the peace of God will be your sentry, your guard, your security unit protecting your heart and mind."**

Simply trust God to take up the issue or matter in your behalf.

SUMMARY

Many of God's people know about spiritual AUTHORITY (#1) ... and about TRANSFER (#3); however, they are missing a floor on the elevator by not implementing RELEASE (#2). They are still embracing the spirit(s) of the demon "loans" who are inviting them to "accept the invitation" and thereby have them "tied" to the situation. Remember, **release is more than forgiveness** ... it also involves **completely divorcing yourself from the situation**. This is one very dangerous omission by modern Christian psychologists and counselors.

Let it go! Forget about it!

I trust this teaching has helped you ... and will continue to help you in the future.

Now ... go help others!

● THINGS TO WATCH FOR

Sometimes you may feel that your life is "out of place" or "out of sync." That is, your walk with the LORD feels different. You know that *"We walk by faith and not by sight;"* however—this is different.

You either feel the "challenge" has left—it's gone somewhere—or you feel like there's nothing left to do (even though you have "tons" of stuff on your plate scheduled to be accomplished).

There are reasons for this. God promised: *"I will instruct you and teach you in the way which you shalt go: I will guide you with my eye (upon you)."* – Psalm 32:8

It is the purpose of this chapter to explain WHY this happens and WHAT to do WHEN it happens.

New things ... new provision.

Things to watch for:

ITEM #1 - When you are tired—weary and worn down—it is important to set aside time to be with God.

Listen to Him and **thank** Him for what He has done for you and yours in the past.

ITEM #2 - When things seem "out of place" it is usually—*assuming we are NOT in sin or rebellion*—that a NEW vista is about to open. **A NEW season**.

Something seems out of place—*different*—because it is like the "freshness" has left (even though you have been productive). It does NOT mean that you are necessarily to stop doing what you have been doing—or even to maintain part(s) of it—but that **a NEW work is about to be assigned to you** ... and **NEW direction**.

A NEW season. That's also where fasting is important.

WARNING: Sometimes this "out of place" feeling can also be because we are about to make a WRONG decision—even one that looks good or advantageous—even to ministry.

We read in 2 Chronicles 25:5-9 ...

> *"Moreover Amaziah gathered Judah together, and made them captains over thousands, and captains over hundreds, according to the houses of their fathers, throughout all Judah and Benjamin: and he numbered them from twenty years old and above, and found them three hundred thousand choice men, able to go forth to war, that could handle spear and shield. He hired also one hundred thousand mighty men of valor*

out of Israel for an hundred talents of silver.

But there came a man of God to him, saying, O king, let not the army of Israel go with you; for the LORD is not with Israel, to wit, with all the children of Ephraim. But if you wilt go, do it, be strong for the battle: God shall make you fall before the enemy: for God has power to help, and to cast down.

*And Amaziah said to the man of God, But what shall we do for all the money I have already given to the army of Israel? And the man of God answered, **The LORD is able to give you much more than this.** "*

God is good not only to lead us—but also to warn us—by His Spirit. In Nehemiah Chapter 8, verse 30, we read: *"[He] testified against them by His Spirit in the prophets."* However, *as a* New Covenant believer in Messiah Jesus you have the Holy Spirit living inside you—you do NOT need a prophet **to guide you**.

However, God may send a prophet to confirm or reveal to you things you are NOT aware of in order to help you make a decision. Like a "spotter" helping his racing team driver in NASCAR; but—*remember*—the driver still has to make the decisions. **You are the driver** ... you are driving your car.

Sometimes **you may be confused** as to whether God is warning you about a bad—*a wrong*—decision you are about to make ... **or whether** ... it is only a "spirit of fear" that is afflicting you. This is easy to discern because **love is stronger than fear**. *"Perfect love casts out all fear."* (1 John 4:18)

"God is a Spirit: and they that worship Him must worship Him in spirit and in truth." (John 4:24) **Speak to the spirit of fear—bind it—and cast it out from disturbing and confusing you in the name of Jesus**. If it leaves, you will know that is what was bothering you. If you still have concerns about the decision, **make sure you do NOT act on the decision unless—*until*—you are sure!** Don't gamble with your future. Remember ... **stay in the peace zone**.

The Holy Spirit will **show us things to come** and **guide us into ALL truth**. (Not just scriptural truth ... but family truth, business truth, etc.) That's WHY we should NOT be too busy in times like this: WAIT, WATCH, LISTEN. (Like the old railroad track signs: "Stop - Look - Listen.")

It all boils down to this: FAITH. You have to draw upon:

- What is in agreement to God's Word;

- How the Holy Spirit is leading you;

- Will the move—or the decision—you are about to make be productive for God's Kingdom;

■ What do you feel in your gut? If you're NOT sure
… then don't.

Your most dangerous enemy is the one you do NOT see!

Ask yourself these questions:

■ Am I living holy?

■ Am I living a "giving" lifestyle?

■ Am I involved in reaching people for Messiah Jesus?

■ Are my motives pure?

If you can answer in the affirmative to these four questions, then know that God will provide for you in whatever decision He leads you. **A NEW thing … and NEW provision**.

> *"Remember you not the former things, neither consider the things of old. Behold, **I will do a new thing**; now it shall spring forth; shall you not know it? **I will even make a way** in the wilderness, and rivers in the desert."* – Isaiah 43:18-19

To help you forge out the powerful future God has ordained for you, I have written three books that will enable you to work hand-in-hand with God: *Faith and*

Quantum Physics ... Total Person Toolbox and Decision Making 101.

● IF YOU'RE NOT SURE … THEN DON'T

Sometimes people get into very difficult, and emotionally trying situations, as a result of a FAST—rash—decision that they make.

It is better to be at peace—to stay in the "peace zone" than to go ahead—even if it looks good!

This can be a trick of the enemy to get you in bondage and mental duress.

Lots of times people are emotionally distressed because of such uncertain behavior: going ahead of God!

This chapter will teach you WHAT to do if you are bound and have lost peace—*that is, you have become emotionally disturbed*—as a result of "going ahead of God."

If you're NOT sure … then don't!

Do NOT make rash decisions.

This is one of the greatest lessons I have learned in life.

Stay in the "peace" zone!!!

When you feel pressured to do something ... if you do NOT have peace about it—WAIT—do NOT go forward.

It is better to be at peace—*to stay in the "peace zone" ... rather than to go ahead*—even if it looks good!

This can be a trick of the enemy to get you in bondage and mental duress.

Pray about the situation. Do NOT let people, even friends, coerce you or persuade you to take action IF you do NOT have peace about the situation.

I promised God one time that I would never do anything, or take action concerning anything, that I was NOT sure about.

If I had a question about the situation, or if I did NOT have peace, I promised God that I would NOT go forward.

The reason I made this promise to God was that I got into a very difficult, and emotionally trying situation, as a result of a FAST—or, rash—decision that I made.

Lots of times people are emotionally distressed because of such uncertain behavior: going ahead of God.

For help with depression, study my teaching, *Healing Mental Disease and Depression*. Also, for healing in different areas of body, mind, or spirit, go to one of my websites: www.hmpodcast.wordpress.com.

Nothing can bind you if you will follow your heart and listen to God.

I am going to tell you WHAT to do if you are bound and have lost peace—*that is if you have become emotionally disturbed*—as a result of "going ahead of God."

- First, PROMISE God that you will NEVER do anything again unless you have peace about it. That is, you will make NO rash decisions. God loves you, my friend, and He does NOT want you bound by unwise decisions and actions. He paid the GREATEST price—the gift of His Son, Messiah Yeshua—that you could be FREE!

- Second, ASK God to turn the situation around and smite Satan through it, and give you a BLESSING in spite of what you have done.

  Ask God for mercy. Read Micah Chapter 7, verses 7 thru 10 in the Tanakh (the Hebrew Old Testament).

- Third, give a GIFT to God. As a result of God turning this situation around, and for His mercy and kindness in restoring you, promise

God AHEAD OF TIME that you will give him a certain, specific gift ... or that you will take a certain, specific action of love and/or sacrifice as a GIFT to Him.

■ Fourth, THANK God ahead of time—and every day—for His deliverance that He is going to show you. He WILL show Himself strong in your behalf IF YOU are sincere.

I trust this teaching will help you, my friend. I learned the SECRET I have shared with you in this chapter the HARD WAY. And through the years, I have seen the manifold mercies of God as a result of what He taught me—even through my RASH decisions—**even decisions that looked good**, or that other people thought were good, **but that I did NOT have peace about when I made them.**

By the way, for some lessons in areas of common every day life, you may want to listen to my "mini" podcasts at: www.princehandley.libsyn.com

Yes, stay in "the zone" where you experience continual freedom: the "peace zone."

Once there, stay there ... don't let anything or anyone get you out of the zone!

And if you need some help with direction, here are some scriptures for you:

- Psalm 27:11

- Jeremiah 42:3

- I Kings 19:9-12

- Isaiah 30:21

ANOINTING FOR SUCCESS ... SLAY GIANTS

Stop worrying about the giants in front of you: the forces, voices and beings that threaten you and keep you from being creative, productive and powerful.

Your enemy, the devil, will lie to you through **people** (even Christians), through **situations**, through your **mind**, through **demons**: he is a master of deception.

Stop concentrating on being broken and start praising and THANKING Jesus for **making you whole**.

Many people have what psychologists label a fear of failure; but I would say—in the people I have counseled through the years—just as many or more have a **fear of success**!

This chapter will teach you not only how to receive the anointing for success ... but how to prepare for *AFTER* your success!

SECRET

Pray AHEAD OF TIME for what you're going to do
AFTER YOUR VICTORY!

Your enemy, the devil, will lie to you through **people** (even Christians), through **situations**, through your **mind**, through **demons**: he is a master of deception.

But I have GOOD NEWS for you. Your Friend Jesus Christ, the Messiah of Israel, will tell you the Truth. He is **The Truth**; His Word is Truth.

Listen to the voice of God. Read His Word and learn from Him. Pray and hear His Spirit.

Stop worrying about the giants in front of you: the forces, voices and beings that threaten you and keep you from being creative, productive and powerful. David had brothers who THOUGHT the giant, Goliath, was too big to fight. **But David THOUGHT the giant was TOO BIG TO MISS!** (1 Samuel 17:47)

How do you SEE your challenges? How do you PERCEIVE them: as obstacles ... or as opportunities? When Moses sent the 12 spies into the Promised Land, the ten men of fear had a different perspective than the two men of faith: Caleb and Joshua. The men of fear saw the people of the land as giants and themselves as grasshoppers in their sight.

The 10 spies gave the people of Israel a bad report of the land, which they had spied out, saying, *"We are NOT able to go up against this people, for they are stronger than we are."* But Caleb said, *"Let us go up at once and* *take possession, for we are well **ABLE** to overcome."* (Numbers 13:30)

The Hebrew word "**able**" used in this passage (**yakol**) means "**to have power, or the capacity to prevail or succeed**." My wonderful mother many times read me the little children's book about the train going up the hill, pulling a load, and saying, "I KNOW I can, I KNOW I can, **I KNOW I can!**"

David succeeded in killing the giant, Goliath, the same way the two men of faith, Caleb and Joshua, succeeded in entering the promise land: because he saw—as they did—**obstacles as opportunities for MIRACLES**: avenues through which God could be glorified! The size of the person is more important than the size of the problem. **Who are you on the inside** and who do you trust!

Do not focus on the giants ... **focus on God**. That is why the enemy lies to you. **The devil wants to get your attention away from your Heavenly Father**: away from God's love for you and His ability to provide for you.

I remember teaching my first born son how to sail. We were in a harbor of the ocean where many yachts and boats were maneuvering. My son kept his attention on another yacht ... what to miss ... instead of our tack (where we should be going). He was focusing on what to miss instead of where to go. So it is with many

Christians: **focusing on the giants instead of the opportunities and goals**.

Stop worrying about whether you are going to sin—and start praising and THANKING God for helping you to **live holy**!

Stop being concerned about failure—and start praising and THANKING God for helping you to **be successful**.

Stop concentrating on being broken—and start praising and THANKING Jesus for **making you whole**. That is why He died on the cross ... but you must appropriate that wholeness by faith.

Pray AHEAD OF TIME for what you're going to do **AFTER** YOUR VICTORY!

Many people have what psychologists label a fear of failure; but I would say—in the people I have counseled through the years—just as many or more have a **fear of success**! King Saul was an example of this. I think he had a fear of success. **Pray AHEAD OF TIME and receive the anointing for what you are going to do AFTER YOUR VICTORY!**

Do not give in and do not give up. If you do NOT quit, you will win! *"I can do ALL things through Christ who strengthens me."* – Philippians 4:13

"With God ALL things are possible." – Matthew 19:26

HOW GOD BRINGS SUCCESS

God has every detail of your life covered.

He is always ready to work for you—and for those people under your tutelage or leadership.

You do NOT need a lot of big programs, you do NOT need a lot of people, and you do NOT need a lot of money.

God can give you a "sign" through your enemies.

This chapter will teach you HOW to overcome fear and sterility in life, business or ministry.

Be watchful for those situations where God can invade the enemy through you and where God will receive ALL the glory!

The Lord can use those situations to bring **deliverance, prosperity, and wholeness to multitudes of people**.

God knows how to win your battle.

Just listen to him!

There are many ways God has to bring you success. Many times He or His angels are working ahead of time—or right on time—in unseen ways to deliver you, to prosper you, and to bring you into a place of super productivity.

Remember, God is FOR YOU. If you ever doubt this, look at the cross. If when we were His enemies, He loved us so much that He sent His only son to die for us, how much more—now that we are His friends—does He want to make us whole in every area of life. [Romans 5:10]

God has every detail of your life covered. If you walk in constant communion with Him—*if the Holy Spirit is your best Friend*—and if you are involved in kingdom work, then you can expect His VERY BEST for you.

At times, the enemy may try to attack you through fear. Fear is a spirit. Fear is the opposite of love. God is love. Perfect love casts out ALL fear. *"There is NO fear in love; but perfect love casts out fear: because fear has torment. He that fears is not made perfect in love."* [1 John 4:18]

Speak to the spirit (demon) of fear; take your authority over it, bind it in Jesus' name and cast it back to the pit of hell.

Use the Word of God against the enemy: *"For God has not given me the spirit of fear; but of power, and of love, and of a sound mind."* [2 Timothy 1:7]

There are times when the devil would try to come against you with a protracted period of fear. This may, or may not, involve people—as agents of the enemy. This is a GOOD SIGN. This tells you that what you are doing—or about to do—is scaring the devil. The enemy is afraid. Since he is a liar, and the father of liars, then you know he is "bluffing you." Don't be afraid to "call his hand" just like you would in a game of poker. The difference is that you're going to use your Heavenly Father's resources (you have the BEST hand!).

In a situation of protracted period of fear, do the following:

Fast;

Wait on God and listen; then,

Do what God tells you.

You may not even have to do anything. The fast may take care of the situation itself. And, remember: If you walk in constant communion with Him—*if the Holy Spirit is your best Friend*—and if you are involved in kingdom work, then you can expect His VERY BEST for you. There are many ways God works for you and many of these are "behind the scenes" operations: "covert" if you will.

GOD IS ALWAYS READY TO WORK FOR YOU

"I will instruct you and teach you in the way you shall go; I will guide you with my eye." [Psalm 32:8]

Realize that this promise is both "individual" and "corporate". God is not only working for YOU, but also for those PEOPLE under your tutelage and leadership. **He wants you to KNOW His deliverance, direction, and dynamics: for your sake, as well as the sake of those people under your watch care.**

To make sure we are the recipients of His instruction, teaching, and guidance we need to be open to His leading and to be Spirit controlled. The verse immediately following the one above tells us, *"Don't be like the horse, or as the mule, which have no understanding, and whose mouths must be held in with bit and bridle."* [Psalm 32:9] This is why we need to be in God's Word every day, talking with Him, listening, and sharing our faith with others: to have understanding of His ways and NOT going our own ways.

GOD WANTS TO WORK FOR YOU IF YOU WILL GIVE HIM THE GLORY

In the Book of Judges, Chapter Six, we read that the children of Israel did evil in the sight of the Lord; and the Lord delivered them into the hand of Midian seven years. Then they cried out to the Lord and, as a result, God raised up a deliverer named Gideon. Gideon had a band of 32,000 people ready to go to war. But God told Gideon, *"The people that are with you are too many for me to give the Midianites into their hands, because [your people] Israel will boast in a vain way saying, 'Our hands won the battle [it wasn't God]'."* [Judges 7:2]

GOD KNOWS HOW TO WIN YOUR BATTLE—JUST LISTEN TO HIM

The Lord told Gideon, *"Whoever is FEARFUL and AFRAID, let him return and depart early ... and 22,000 people returned; and there remained 10,000."* Next, the Lord told Gideon, "The people are still too many." God then had Gideon separate the remaining people into two groups, depending upon how they drank water: if they bowed down upon their knees, or if they put their hand to their mouth and lapped the water with their tongues as a dog laps. God then told Gideon he would save them by the 300 men that lapped, and the other 9,700 were sent home.

You see, God wants to receive the glory for what He does through you, my friend. **You do NOT need a lot of big programs, you do NOT need a lot of people, and you do NOT need a lot of money.** You just need the

Spirit of God anointing you and directing you as you obey what He instructs you to do.

GOD CAN GIVE YOU A SIGN THROUGH YOUR ENEMIES

That same night the Lord told Gideon to go down to the host of the enemy because he was going to deliver them into Gideon's hands. The Lord told Gideon, *"But if you are AFRAID to go down, then take your servant with you and you shall hear what the enemy says."* One of the enemy soldiers had a dream and Gideon heard him tell another soldier about the dream. The soldier said the dream was about Gideon, a man of Israel, *"for into his hand God has delivered us [Midian and all the host]."*

That is exactly what happened! That night the Lord gave Gideon and his band of men a GIANT victory. Gideon had only 300 men and they defeated the Midianites and the Amalekites and all the children of the East who were in the valley like grasshoppers in multitude; and their camels were without number, as the sand by the sea side for multitude. [Judges 7:12]

Remember: one person plus God is a MAJORITY!

Be watchful for those situations where God can invade the enemy through you and where God will receive ALL the glory! The Lord can use those situations to bring **deliverance, prosperity, and**

wholeness to multitudes of people. And God will be glorified because everyone will know you could never do these things on your own: they are MIRACLES!

"But thanks be unto God, which gives us the victory through our Lord Jesus Christ." [1 Corinthians 15:57]

TRIANGLE OF SUCCESS: THREEFOLD CORD

What would you like to attain for the Lord in your ministry, your life, your family, or your business that you have not been able to attain in the past?

There are three (3) things that can make you MORE SUCCESSFUL ... or break you.

It's easy to be hurt in the fast paced world we live in today; but even in tribal areas where I have ministered there is hurt and hatred; sometimes decades and centuries old.

In this chapter you will learn about relational space—and about associations. Also, you will **learn about what "signs" to watch for in negative circumstances** that prove you are on the right track.

There are simple "examinations" you may make that will put you on the right track for success from God—and help you maintain that position.

By learning and observing the "threefold cord" in this book you will be strategically positioned for—and guaranteed—success!

What would you like to attain for the Lord in your ministry, your life, your family, or your business that you have not been able to attain in the past?

What is on your wish list?

What would you change about your present situation?

What are your pains and unfulfilled wants?

The Psalms minister to us to help and direct, as well as to evoke worship. Psalm 37:4 says, *"Delight thyself also in the Lord, and He shall give thee the desires of thine heart."*

The Hebrew word for "**delight**" is "**anag**" and **it means to be "pliable" and also to "delight yourself."** In other words ... ENJOY the MESSIAH. Have fun with the Lord, and don't be so tight or bound up that you can't express pleasurable emotion toward Him. If you enjoy him and have pleasurable emotion toward Him, He will grant you the petitions of your inner most being, even your thoughts and intellect.

No matter how much you've been used by God in the past ... no matter how much Bible knowledge and training you have ... and no matter how much favor you have with people, **there are three (3) things that can make you MORE SUCCESSFUL or break you:**

Friends;
Thoughts; and,
Time.

The Holy Bible tells us: *"And if one prevail against him, two shall withstand him; and a threefold cord is not quickly broken."* [Ecclesiastes 4:12]

Learn to ENJOY the Lord and to engage yourself positively in the three (3) areas above.

FRIENDS

Who are your close friends and associates? Do they contribute to your intellectual and spiritual well being?

There are four (4) types of relational space:

> Public;

> Social;

> Personal; and,

> Intimate.

Public space is usually the space that's 12 feet and beyond. But it can be as close as the cashier at the grocery store. In an elevator it might be closer.

Social space is usually four to 12 feet and would normally be experienced at settings like school or social activities. Eye contact and gestures help feed it.

Personal space is usually 18 inches to 4 feet and normally found in friendship type relationships.

Intimate space can be from touching to 18 inches and is usually experienced with someone who knows the challenging aspects of your life. There is also "naked" space which refers to "emotional" space. This is a relationship, or situation, where your level of vulnerability is very high.

Today, there is a lot of teaching, and many books being written, on the subject of mentoring. However, **remember that Jesus is the only perfect mentor**. He is a friend that sticks closer than a brother! It's easy to be hurt in the fast-paced world we live in today; but even in tribal areas where I have ministered there is hurt and hatred; sometimes decades and centuries old.

In the USA there has long been a series of stories, songs, and cartoons about the Hatfields and McCoys, feuding families in the hill country. Many people think it is a fictional story made up by writers; however, it is true. In 1878 Randolph Hatfield allegedly stole a pig (swine) from the McCoy family. Eleven (11) people were killed in the 10 years between 1882 and 1892. Recently, after 125 years, the two families signed a document—a covenant before Almighty God—publicly forgiving and releasing each other.

Proverb 13:20 tells us, *"He that walks with wise men shall be wise: but a companion of fools shall be destroyed."* I am sure you know this already, but **examine your friendships**.

Do NOT associate closely with those who have a problem with anger, laziness, talk too much, or are loose with their morals.

Also, **do NOT associate with those people who keep reminding you of past sins** you've already dealt with and for which you've asked forgiveness. They may even be relatives, or those who have been in close relational space as outlined above. **These people are doing what God won't even let Satan do: they are going beyond the BLOOD of Christ**.

The whole intent of the devil using them—even though they may not be cognizant of it—is to put you into a negative spin, to bring you down from the heavenly places (*Colossians* Chapter Three). **It is the devil's attempt to take you back into a place from which you have been forgiven, cleansed, and delivered!**

A reality check for the future: look at your friends. **Associate with other dreamers!** I would rather be alone with Jesus than to be with someone who didn't motivate and encourage me. I want to be with people who sharpen my skills and intellect ... who "fan my flames" and enlarge my vision. Three of the greatest inventors the USA has produced used to spend recreational time together in the woods and on picnics: Thomas Edison, Harvey Firestone, and Henry Ford.

Associate with the right people. If you don't have anyone with which to associate, then email me your dreams and aspirations, or your problems. I will be glad to share with you. We are all working on the same team with the same goals. Send your email to: PrinceHandley@gmail.com.

THOUGHTS

Whether you realize it or not, **you are moving in the direction of your thoughts.**

Proverb 23:7 tells us *"For as he thinks in his heart so is he."* The Hebrew word here for "**thinks**" is "**shaar**" and is a primitive root **which means "to split or open" and to act as a "gatekeeper."** Don't open your mind to every thought that comes along! Satan is a liar and the father of lies [John 8:44] and **Satan has a mind oriented strategy to kill you, to steal from you, and to destroy you** [John 10:10]. **The devil has two main weapons: deception and lies.**

Your thoughts, like dreams, can **come from three (3) sources: God, yourself, or the enemy**.

If you believe lies from Satan—*or accusations from people*—then you put barriers in your life. Do NOT dwell on them, but realize their source. Defamation of character and an evil report—especially after a person has repented and asked for forgiveness—is out of the pit of hell. It is one of the things that is an abomination to God. [Proverbs 6:16-19]

Do not be a part of defamation of character. If someone is attacking you in such a manner, then pray and ask God what you should do about it. He may not have you do anything about it, as the accuser will be severely dealt with by the Holy Spirit.

God still has GOOD things for you. **When one door closes, God always has a NEW ONE!**

"For I know the thoughts that I think toward you, says the Lord, thoughts of peace and not of evil, to give you a future and a hope." [Jeremiah 29:11]

Let God's thoughts fill your mind with life, hope, and positivity. Dwell on creative aspects of life and ministry.

"Casting down imaginations, and every high thing that exalts itself against the knowledge of God, and bringing into captivity every thought to the obedience of Christ." [2 Corinthians 10:5]

Refuse to retreat. Ask God to give you NEW IDEAS, new thoughts, and creative imagination to reach the world for Messiah. Sometimes I tape large blank sheets of paper 27 by 34 inches (68.6 by 86.4 cm) on my walls just to write down new ideas to reach nations and people for Messiah Yeshua. I have found that either **just after, or during, a major attack from the enemy, the Lord usually blesses me with dynamic ideas** for reaching mass multitudes with the Good News of Messiah.

So when negative thoughts or attacks come my way, they are a "sign" that the enemy is scared, trying to discourage me and get me on a negative bent. The enemy, being a spirit being, probably can recognize an anointing building up—ideas that will be formulated in my mind by the Holy Spirit—which will do great damage to the kingdom of darkness. Therefore, I rejoice for the glory of God that will soon be manifest to people in the tribes and families of the world! How great is our God?!

I encourage you to do the same; **never back up ... stand still and listen to God's directions ... then advance ... and SEE the salvation of the Lord**.

When the children of Israel were trapped by the Red Sea with Pharaoh and 600 chosen chariots of war hot on their heels, Moses said to them:

"Do not be afraid. STAND STILL, and see the salvation of the Lord, which He will accomplish for you today. For

the Egyptians whom you see today, you shall see again no more forever.

The Lord will fight for you, and you shall hold your peace.

And the Lord said to Moses, 'Why do you cry to me? Tell the children of Israel to GO FORWARD'." [Exodus 14:13-15]

Hundreds of years later, Jahaziel prophesied to the children of Israel with similar instructions from the Lord:

"You will not need to fight in this battle. Position yourselves, STAND STILL and see the salvation of the Lord, who is with you, O Judah and Jerusalem! Do not fear or be dismayed: tomorrow GO OUT AGAINST THEM, for the Lord is with you." [2 Chronicles 20:16-17]

TIME

Previously I discussed the importance of time. We learned that **we need the Holy Spirit to anoint our time**. Our lives are made up of basic segues of days, in between which we sleep and obtain rest from the Lord. And, every seventh day is ordained from the Lord to bless us as a day of rest. [Isaiah 58]

During our waking hours we need to spend quality time talking to the Holy Spirit. The Bible depicts the Spirit as a dove. In Israel the dove was the turtle dove: a beautiful symbol of love, peace, gentleness, and innocence.

"And John bare record, saying, I saw the Spirit descending from heaven like a dove, and it abode upon Him (Jesus)." [John 1:32]

To understand the Holy Spirit more, we should **learn what a turtle dove is like**.

> Turtle doves never fight. Pigeons do.
>
> Turtle doves don't like noise. Pigeons do.
>
> Turtle doves like to be alone. Pigeons like crowds.
>
> Turtle doves are not territorial. Pigeons "bully" each other.
>
> Turtle doves can't be trained or domesticated. Pigeons can be.
>
> Turtle doves mate for life. Pigeons often have multiple partners.

Now if you want to be close to the Holy Spirit, to have wonderful communion with Him, observe His ways. Then, **prepare a nesting place in your heart for the Holy Spirit!** Spend quality time with Him. The more you honor Him, the more He will honor you!

The Holy Spirit is God's agent on earth to supply the resurrection power of Christ!

Learn to ENJOY the Lord so He can give you the desires of your heart. Engage yourself positively and wisely with:

Your **friends**;

Your **thoughts**; and,

Your **time** of fellowship with the Holy Spirit.

I pray this teaching will help you. Now you know the formula: **The Triangle of Success**.

APOSTOLIC MIRACLE MINISTRY – MIRACLES FOLLOW YOU

Apostleship did NOT end with the early apostles. Miracles—real miracles—did NOT end with the early apostles.

You are NOT going to reach many "New Age" people without MIRACLES! You are NOT going to reach many Jewish people without MIRACLES! You are NOT going to reach many Muslims without MIRACLES!

This chapter is for BOTH those **who believe in miracles** AND those **who do not believe in miracles**.

God never intended for us to be impotent representatives of the Kingdom of God.

I remember a lady who was heavily involved in New Age religion. I prayed for her and she was healed instantly of a condition she had for years. She said *"You have POWER!"* I explained to her that I didn't have power, but it was Jesus who loved her. He is the WAY to eternal life: the ONLY WAY!

There are THREE (3) precepts necessary to enable you to have a more productive healing and miracle ministry. They are very simple and not only will you be a greater blessing to many on earth ... but eternity will manifest the extreme **multiplied** fruit of your compassion. You will learn these three precepts in this chapter.

Have an exciting life of MIRACLES with Jesus, the Messiah!

God never intended for us to be impotent representatives of the Kingdom of God.

Jesus taught his disciples, *"Go into all the world and preach the gospel to every creature—and these signs shall FOLLOW them that believe."* [Mark 16:15-18]

"And they went forth, and preached everywhere, the Lord working with them, and confirming the word with signs FOLLOWING." [Mark 16:20]

"The Jews seek (require) a sign." [1 Corinthians 1:22]

"For I am the LORD; I change NOT." [Malachi 3:6]

"Jesus Christ, the SAME: yesterday, and today, and forever." [Hebrews 13:8]

This section is for BOTH those **who believe in miracles** AND those **who do not believe in miracles**.

God never intended for us to be impotent representatives of the Kingdom of God. He has NEVER changed His plan of salvation and never will. *"I am the LORD; I change not."* [Malachi 3:6]

Are you afraid that God will not come through for you the next time you pray for a sick friend? **Pray anyway!** Are you concerned about who will get the blame if the prayer is not answered? Will it be God's fault—or will it be your fault—or will it be the sick person's fault?

There are THREE (3) precepts necessary to enable you to have a more productive healing and miracle ministry. They are very simple ... follow these precepts and not only will you be a greater blessing to many on earth ... but eternity will manifest the extreme fruit of your compassion. We will now discuss these three precepts.

PRECEPT #1 - BELIEVE

"If you can BELIEVE; all things are possible if you believe." [Mark 9:23] Another translation of this verse is: *"If you can? BELIEVE! All things are possible if you believe."* (Read the context.) *"All things whatsoever you shall ask in my name BELIEVING, you shall receive."* To help you BELIEVE, study scriptures on healing. Find a concordance and read all the Bible verses on healing, heal, healed, etc. Also, for a short scripture by scripture presentation on healing, go to: www.realmiracles.org/how-to-be-healed.html You may want to memorize these scriptures.

Also, read and study carefully the book, *Health and Healing Complete Guide to Wholeness*. It covers:

Different avenues of healing;

How to receive healing;

How to be an instrument of healing for others; and,

Hindrances to healing (different reasons why people are not healed).

If your HEART is right before God—and if you have the DESIRE—you can become a MIRACLE WORKING bearer of the Good News! *"What things you DESIRE, when you PRAY, BELIEVE that you RECEIVE them; and YOU SHALL HAVE THEM."* [Mark 11:24]

"And ALL things, whatsoever you shall ask in prayer, BELIEVING, you shall receive." [Matthew 21:22] Stop being concerned about HOW MUCH faith you have. **If you only have faith the size of a small seed—just USE IT**. Loose (release) that faith in the NAME of JESUS. *"Whatever you ask the Father in my name, He will give it to you—ask, and you shall receive."* [John 16:23-24]

PRECEPT #2 - BE COMMISSIONED

"You go therefore, and teach ALL nations, baptizing them in the name of the Father, and of the Son, and of

the Holy Ghost: teaching them to observe ALL things whatsoever I have commanded you: and, remember, I am with you ALWAYS unto the end of the world." [Matthew 28:19-20] This commission was given to the apostles with the mandate that they were to "teach them—*the ones they were discipling and training*—ALL things whatsoever I have commanded you." The phrase **"all things" includes**, of course, **the commissioning or sending out of other workers and apostles**.

Mark 13:10 tells us: *"This Good News of the kingdom will be preached in ALL the earth, and then will the end come."* **That commission is ongoing until the "end of the age,"** or world, and the Kingdom of Heaven is continually being perpetuated like yeast used in sourdough bread —*or added bacteria used in starting yogurt*—only with GREAT MULTIPLICATION.

Apostleship did NOT end with the early apostles. Ephesians 4:11-12 tells us that God placed apostles, prophets, evangelists, pastors and teachers in the Body of Christ *"to equip the saints for the work of the ministry ... for building up the body of Christ."* **Nowhere do we ever read in the Holy Bible where God ever terminated these offices of pastors, teachers, evangelists, prophets and apostles**. The Body of Messiah (real born again believers in Christ, both dead and alive) is NOT—**and will not**—be built up fully (completely) until the completion of the Church when she is "caught up" and meets Messiah Jesus in the air. [1 Thessalonians 4;17]

NOTICE:

Many Bible teachers promote the view that the five-fold ministries were terminated after the Early Church era. The reason they propound this view is because these ministry offices do NOT function in their lives—AND the gifts of the Holy Spirit do NOT operate in their lives. It is a clever excuse for "neutered" and powerless ministry. Many rabbis and pastors and teachers have been taught this by their mentors and teachers (who also minister without power). After all, you get what you believe!

An "apostle" is basically a "sent one." In early Greek literature the word "apostello" was used to describe a ship leaving its port with its goods and a bill of lading, headed for its destination. [For example: a ship leaving its port in North Africa headed for Greece.] As soon as the ship was unloaded, and having delivered its wares and products, it was labeled "apostello," an "apostle" ship: a "sent one."

Notice, you do NOT have to be an apostle— which is one of the ministry gifts to the church—[see again Ephesians 4:11-12] to be commissioned. Part of Christ's commission to the early apostles was to *"go into ALL the world and preach the gospel"*—AND—to *"teach them [the new believers who follow through with water baptism]* **all things** *whatsoever I have commanded you."* **"All things" includes the mandate to** *"Go into* **ALL the world."** It is a self perpetuating movement from the moment our Lord pronounced it! Nothing has stopped it, nothing is stopping it, and nothing ever will stop it!

Ask your church or fellowship to lay hands on you and send you out. You might want to spend a time of prayer and fasting before this. **NOTE: Beware if your church says it is going to "release" you!** You're NOT in bondage! Too many churches are "releasing" ministry instead of "sending" ministry!!! To be "sent out" or "commissioned" does NOT mean necessarily that you will be changing geographic locality (unless, of course, the Spirit of God directs you in this matter). You may well remain, for a season—or for the rest of your life—in your present locality bearing fruit for Christ as one "sent out" and ministering from and for the body of Christ, the Church.

Above all, **make sure it is a POWER church or synagogue which commissions you**: one whose leaders believe in the five-fold ministry offices, and where the gifts of the Holy Spirit operate in and through its members.

The mark of a productive Spirit filled church or synagogue is regular SPIRIT DIRECTED training, prayer support and sending out—THE

COMMISSIONING—of workers for Messiah Jesus. If you want to WIN in life ... then give your life to Messiah Jesus and line up with His commission!

More and more, as we near the time of Messiah's return, we will also see the sending out—the commissioning—of workers to Israel and the Jewish People, and the subsequent planting of Messianic houses of worship. These will only be fully productive and have the FULL BLESSING of God as they shed the exclusivism manifest in so many Messianic fellowships and synagogues today!

Jesus INCLUDES. A spirit of exclusivism is NOT contributory to Yeshua's ministry of compassion, love, and MIRACLES.

PRECEPT #3 - GO WITH GOOD NEWS

"Go into all the world and preach the gospel to every creature—And **these signs shall follow them that believe.***"* [Mark 16:15-18] If you GO ... signs will follow. Let me repeat: **signs FOLLOW them that believe! You have to GO before something can FOLLOW you!**

Take the opportunity to pray for people when it appears (when you are aware of their need) ... unless the Spirit of God prompts you not to. There are several reasons for this which we will cover at a later time in another book.

Covenant with God that you will take each opportunity presented to you to **pray for the physical needs of people in the next seven days**. It will change your life and help bring healing and deliverance for many people. **You don't have to be miracle conscious ... just be JESUS conscious!** You don't have to be a preacher. You don't have to have the "gift" of healing (although there is such a gift). You don't have to have the "gift" of faith (although there is such a gift).

I love to pray for Jews. As far as I know I have never prayed for a Jewish person to be healed that was not healed. Also, as far as I know I have never prayed for a Jewish person for anything that the request was NOT answered! I give ALL the credit to the Ruach HaChodesh (the Holy Spirit). **Pray for Jews as the LORD gives you the opportunity. It will greatly ENRICH your personal life and your walk with the LORD.** In addition, God will BLESS YOU in a special way. *"I will bless them that bless you, and I will curse them that curse you."* [Genesis 12:3]

Take the opportunities. Pray for Muslims, pray for Jews, pray for those ensnared or blinded in the New Age movement. Most of the people in the New Age movement and in false religions are really nice people who are seeking the WAY of life, but who have been deceived by the god of this world. I remember a lady who was heavily involved in New Age religion. I prayed for her and she was healed instantly of a condition she had for years. She said *"You have POWER!"* I explained to her that I didn't have power, but it was Jesus who loved her. He is the WAY to eternal life: the ONLY WAY!

**IF YOUR PLANS FIT INTO GOD'S PLANS
YOU WILL HAVE GOD'S FAITH
AND GOD'S FAITH ALWAYS WORKS!**

I pray this teaching will help you. Have an exciting life of MIRACLES with the Lord Jesus!

THE BLESSING – NO CURSE

Many of God's People are clandestinely held back from their maximum potential by not only a lack of stretching out in faith—but also by focusing on the negatives instead of the positives. They are in defensive mode. Just as in sports, the BEST defense is a GOOD OFFENSE!

The root of ALL curses on Planet Earth originated with the sin of disobedience by Adam. The Messiah of Israel became a curse for us that we might be blessed. He took on Him—*at the cross-stake*—the curse that originated with Adam in the Garden of Eden.

This chapter will teach you HOW to receive the BLESSING with its PROTECTION from the administrative unit of the Throne of Heaven.

Of utmost importance to the reader will be the knowledge of HOW to enjoin the legal injunction of BLESSING and PROTECTION for your family and all that God has given you—*even in the future*—by birth, adoption and assignment.

Receive the blessing—*with its protection*—from the administrative unit of God's throne in Heaven.

If you know Jesus Christ and are baptized in His wonderful Spirit, **you do not have to succumb to oppositions and attacks**. In 50 years of ministry I have found that many Christians are clandestinely held back from their maximum potential by not only a lack of stretching out in faith **...** but also **by focusing on the negatives instead of the positives**. They are in defensive mode. Just as in sports, the BEST defense is a GOOD OFFENSE!

On the cross, Jesus (Yeshua) became a curse for us that we might receive the blessings of Abraham. Notice, **the Messiah of Israel became a curse for us that we might be blessed**. He took on Him—*at the cross-stake*—the curse that originated with Adam in the Garden of Eden. **He took ALL curses that are encompassed by that disobedience of our first father: the first man, the first Adam**.

The root of ALL curses on Planet Earth originated with the sin of disobedience by Adam in the Garden of Eden when he disobeyed God and obeyed Satan. When Adam did this, he relinquished his ruler-ship of Planet Earth and yielded it to the Evil One. Notice, **there is NOT a curse on earth that does NOT originate as a result of that ONE ACT of disobedience!**

In Genesis Chapter 3 we read of a prophecy concerning the Seed of the first woman, Eve. Her seed would defeat, destroy, and subjugate the tempter, Satan, who deceived Adam in the Garden of Eden. This prophecy was pertaining to the 2nd Adam, the Son of God—the Mashiach of Israel—who would come to delete the curse and install the blessing(s) which were already programmed before the foundation of the world: the BLESSINGS originating from GOD.

You were redeemed with the precious BLOOD of Christ, who was as of a lamb without blemish and without spot, and who truly was **foreordained before the foundation of the world**, but was manifest in these last times for you. The BLESSING was PLANNED FOR YOU before God created the world.

The universe was created for Planet Earth, and Planet Earth was created for YOU! The ROOT of ALL blessing(s) ON EARTH—*and ultimately in Heaven*—was purchased by Christ FOR YOU on the cross-stake through His shed BLOOD ... and thereby deleting the curse. **Through His resurrection He installed the blessing**.

It was the first man, Adam, who initiated the curse through DISOBEDIENCE to God. It took another man—the God man, who was God's Son—to delete the curse through OBEDIENCE to God **so that we (mankind) could be BLESSED.**

In the window of time between the fall of man in the garden—*with the resultant CURSE*—and the death and resurrection of Christ—*with the resultant LEGAL installation of the BLESSING*—**God made a WAY for man to APPROPRIATE His blessing(s)**. That WAY was the same process by which men, women, and children appropriate God's blessing(s) today: the WAY of FAITH.

Enoch, Abraham, Sarah, Deborah, Joseph, Moses, Elijah, Elisha, Daniel—and many others—appropriated the blessing(s) through faith. Read Hebrews Chapter 11.

In Genesis 12:1-3 God told Abraham: *"And I will make of you a great nation, and I will bless you, and make your name great; and you shall be a blessing: and I will bless them that bless you, and curse him that curses you; and in you shall all the families of the earth be blessed."* Later, in Genesis 22:18 God told Abraham: *"In thy seed shall all nations of the earth be blessed. Because you have obeyed my voice."*

The SEED of Abraham (the Messiah Jesus) became a curse FOR US that we might be blessed with faithful Abraham. The SEED (Messiah Jesus) broke ALL the curse(s)—even the ROOT of the curse(s) imposed in the garden of Eden with the resultant sin, death, effects of witchcraft, sins of the father, generational curse(s)—so that ALL people could be FREE from the curse(s) and be recipients of the blessing(s).

Christ (Messiah) has redeemed us from the curse of the law, being made a curse for us: For It is written, *"Cursed is everyone that hangs on a tree, so that the BLESSING of Abraham might come on the non-Jews (Gentiles) through Messiah Jesus."* (Galatians 3:13-14)

Romans 4:13 tells us: *"The promise that he (Abraham) should be the heir of the world, was NOT to Abraham, or to his seed, through the law, but through the righteousness of FAITH."* **Just as God works through FAITH, the enemy of your soul works through FEAR.** The MIRACLES of God—salvation, healing, power, tongues, commissioning—all work through FAITH. The evils of Satan—witchcraft, disease, spiritual impotence, confusion—all work through fear.

The BLOOD of Christ is your covering! The BLOOD will protect you from the works of the enemy. The BLOOD of Christ is living. The life of God is in THE BLOOD. The enemy can NOT come beyond the blood line. In Revelation 12:11 we read: *"They overcame him [the devil] by the BLOOD of the Lamb, and by the word of their testimony, and they loved not their lives unto the death."* If the BLOOD is your covering, you are protected.

Every day remember to speak (declare) the BLOOD of Christ over yourself, your family, your property, and everything the Lord has placed in your hands by birth, adoption or assignment—and the domains over which you preside.

A good Jewish friend of mine, Rachmiel Frydland, would sneak into the Warsaw Nazi concentration camp during World War II. Rachmiel was Jewish and he would sneak into the camp and declare the Gospel and then sneak back out. He prayed with many of his Jewish brethren who received Yeshua as their Messiah before they were murdered: the very next day after he was there! I had the privilege to be in his home several times and to have wonderful fellowship with him. Rachmiel knew the importance of the BLOOD of Jesus.

Do not worry about any generational curses or curses from the bloodline of your relatives and forefathers. BREAK THEM with the BLOOD of CHRIST! Do not fear about some witch or someone placing a curse on you—fear is a tool of the enemy. The Holy Bible says, *"The curse causeless shall NOT come."* If you have done something wrong then confess it to God, ask for forgiveness and cover yourself with the HOLY BLOOD of CHRIST.

You are God's property and the BLOOD of Christ is your COVERING if you will declare it so in faith. Enjoin the blood of the covenant. Instruct THE BLOOD to be applied to yourself and situations BY FAITH. Prohibit the enemy and his people or demons from performing an action against you or your loved ones by your SPOKEN injunction of FAITH. **It is a legal injunction purchased by the Lord Jesus Christ on the cross and imposed by your faith.** ATTACH The Blood, JOIN The Blood,

IMPOSE The Blood to yourself, your loved ones, and to your situations.

Request of the Father in Heaven to cover you and your situations with the BLOOD of CHRIST. In the name of Jesus verbally charge the enemy AND his power to be broken off your life and your situations. **It is a direct command with authority.** You have the POWER in the name of JESUS to exercise authoritative—or dominating control or influence—over the devil and his works of darkness. Jesus purchased this power for you, and commissioned you with this apostolic power to go:

> Preach and teach the Good News;
> Heal the sick; and,
> Cast out demons.

Be FREE from doubt. Believe in the abilities and power the Lord Jesus has purchased for you by His death and resurrection!

You have been granted this power inherently by THE BLESSING from the administrative unit of the throne of Heaven. This is POWER delegated from Heaven to you! **The blessings of Abraham are yours.** You rule as a king in life through Jesus Christ.

● DIE TO COMFORT ZONES: RECEIVE MIRACLE RESULTS

Many of God's People are "tied" to their present level of blessing and productivity like the monkey who held onto the banana in the jar ... and couldn't get the banana out to enjoy it. They are "locked" into their comfort zones.

It is very threatening to think about leaving our comfort zones—*possibly making potential sacrifices*—**unless we realize the profit and the productivity that WILL result from the promise**.

I say "promise" because Jesus taught, *"Except a grain of wheat falls into the ground and die, it abides alone: but if it dies, it brings forth much fruit."* [John 12:24]

What is it that God is asking YOU to DIE TO at this point of your life or ministry?

In this chapter you will learn real life experience of what happens when you obey God and die to your seeming comfort zone.

You will read about MIRACLE results: the profit and productivity that results from the PROMISE.

It can happen to YOU—*and will*—if you will listen to God and obey Him!

Jesus taught, *"Except a grain of wheat falls into the ground and dies, it abides alone: but if it dies, it will bring forth much fruit."* [John 12:24]

What is it that God is asking YOU to DIE TO at this point of your life and ministry?

If YOU will DIE to that thing, or to those things, about which God is speaking TO YOU, you will see increased productivity: resurrection power!

My family of five lived in a little 22 foot by 22 foot house (I have over twice the children now). There was one bedroom and I even disposed of the bed so I could use the bedroom for an office. (Volunteer workers would come over and work in the other part of the house.)

My family and I were sleeping on the floor at night. The children were little and sometimes they would wet the bed (the floor!) while sleeping. I decided I was going to do something about this. That is, **let God do something about it!**

After praying, the Lord laid it upon my heart to give a certain portion (offering) above my tithe to Him for six (6) months. The offering amount was a very high portion: **higher than I had ever given**. During those months I would get up before dawn and write down Bible verses on cards, then memorize them and record them onto cassettes. **I DIED to both the comfort of sleep and the comfort of only giving my usual offering amount above the tithe**.

At the end of the six months I was instructed of the Lord to leave that place (I really liked it—it was my comfort zone) and take my family with me to another state far away. When I arrived there, I located my family in a nice place to stay and decided to get alone for a while in a previously used animal shed on a farm in a rural area.

I locked myself into the shed and instructed that no one should come see me or contact me because I wanted to fast and be alone with the Lord. **I took in enough water to last for 40 days**. I shut myself in, making sure the door and all windows were locked and covered, making it impossible for anyone to come in or to see in.

After a few days I heard footsteps approaching the shed in the barn. I had instructed my family that nobody was to come there or to try to contact me. I just wanted to be alone with God. When I heard the footsteps I even placed a chair against the door (even though it was locked) to make sure nobody could enter. Then, I heard the footsteps walk away; there was no knock and no voice.

Later, I looked under the chair and saw an envelope. **When I opened it I found $75,000 USD**. I didn't know what to do … except praise God!!! **I stayed another few days and the same thing happened, only this time** there was **$25,000 USD. That made a total of $100,000 dollars US!** I talked to God about it: I said, *"God, I know I promised you I would be with here for 40 days, but I think I need to go to the bank!"*

No, I did NOT sell my soul. Actually, God understood and used this money to keep me from serious damage to my body. The animal shed where I was fasting had just been painted before I locked myself in, and I would have been seriously injured internally (poisoned) had I stayed there longer. **God not only used the money to bless me, but also to get me out of the place to protect my body from harm.** As it was, I had some bad effects later from just the few days I was there fasting and breathing fumes.

I died to my comfort zone of a home where I was reaching nations and where I had lived for a few years: where people knew me and where the ministry was centered; and **God brought resurrection power plus a great increase in productivity to many nations, tribes, and peoples … and it is still happening!**

I was able to purchase printing equipment that helped me reach many more thousands of people in many languages, and to travel overseas to nations with the Good News! Many new churches have been raised up through the literature we have published through the years.

We also bought time and put programs on different radio stations in different geographic areas for 40 consecutive broadcasts (five days a week for 8 weeks) and offered $36 in FREE Bible audio teachings to anyone who would write. They have gone around the world in the last 40 years and ended up in far away villages in other countries; and eventually led us into the multi-channel audio casts we do today.

Miracles—real miracles—were experienced by people as they listened to these broadcasts. One man wrote us and said as he was driving down the highway **he put his hand on the radio and it felt like electricity was going through his body as he was instantly healed**.

What is God asking YOU to DIE TO? Is it that power play down at the office ... is it your impatience or your ego ... OR is it that interpersonal relationship at your church or ministry?

What is it about which the Lord is or has been dealing with you? Is it a person or thing? I promise you on the authority of God's Holy Word that if YOU will DIE to that person or thing, God will bring forth resurrection life!

Pray NOW—obey God, and yield to Him. **Die to that situation, person, or thing ... and then watch God bring resurrection life—increased productivity—and multiply it around the world!**

Remember, the Holy Spirit is God's agent on earth to supply the resurrection power of Christ!

I know this teaching will help you experience miracles, increased productivity and resurrection power.

GLOBAL EVANGELISM SECRETS

The Gospel is not only cross-cultural—it is omni-cultural. There is always ONE benchmark to apprise whether we are effectively reaching any culture: **the cross-stake.**

In the world—and nations in particular—there are many cultures and sometimes micro cultures. Within each culture there are subcultures. Sometimes these subcultures overlap national and ethnic boundaries.

There are different **TRENDS** throughout the years and throughout your lifetime and ministry. There are different **TIMES** of refreshing as well as seasons of opportunity. There are different ministries as well as gifts of the Holy Spirit—but only **ONE LORD.**

This chapter is a basic primer for social media evangelism and is designed to give the reader examples of trends in media, generational cultures and suggestions for practical outreach. **It is not designed to replace what you may be doing, but to provide NEW ideas** through practical examples and suggestions.

Resources are also included to help the reader help others!

Especially helpful to the person engaged in Global Evangelism and Church Planting are **tips pertaining to protection and power while you are working on special projects for the LORD.**

For **advanced mission strategies** the reader should consult the following two books by Prince Handley:

> *The Art of Christian Warfare*; and,

> *New Global Strategy.*

The Millennials—define a core of beliefs as to life style and generally fall into the age group of 28 to 38 (during 2017 to 2020).

God is eternally young. He is NOT some old man with a long beard sitting in a rocking chair!

The Gospel is not only cross-cultural—it is omni-cultural. There is always ONE benchmark to apprise whether we are effectively reaching any culture: **the cross-stake.**

One time, after preaching to the usual mega audience, Billy Graham felt discouraged because he sensed a lack of power during the message. A close associate told him, *"Billy, you forgot the cross!"*

In the world, and nations in particular, there are many cultures and sometimes micro cultures. Within each culture there are subcultures. Sometimes these subcultures overlap national and ethnic boundaries. For example, age stratification: a specific example of which would be youth. The micro cultures within these sub cultures constantly change; some over long periods of time, usually in less civilized, less advanced societies.

TRENDS

An example of a micro culture would be the age groups in Western and some European cultures labeled Generation "Y" (or those attempting to emulate them). Baby Boomers were born in the post WW II years of 1946 thru 1955, with a later generation from 1955 through 1965 referred to as Generation Jones.

Generation X'ers were born after the Post WW II baby boom, from the early 1960's through early 1980's.

Generation Y spends more on consumer goods than GEN 13, and because of their numbers, GEN 13 (Millennials) are the targets of major marketing strategies. They are STIMULATED by more information, and more options, and situations that require decision making. They are often accused of growing up too fast. **What a PERFECT segment of society to reach with the message of the CROSS and then train to reach the world in these days before the return of Messiah.**

GEN 13—also referred to as The Millennials—define a core of beliefs as to life style and generally fall into the age group of 28 to 38 (during 2017 through 2020). **Many in this group grew up in their grandparents' homes**

as a result of their parents' divorce. They know how to make a fast decision based upon pragmatics, especially in the area of economics and money—but can easily perceive the truth and value of the Good News when presented to them with love and sincerity. **Prince Handley believes this is a KEY segment to evangelize for entry into the Last Days.**

Also, Prince Handley believes the greatest segment to evangelize NOW and in the future is under 15 years of age. The mass of the population (over 50 percent) in nations is under the age of 15. If you reach the young people, you will effectively:

1. Reach the next generation and future leaders;

2. Reach those who will have the longest lifetime of service for the LORD.

3. Reach the greatest amount of people.

NOTE: Use the *Wordless Book* you can find here: www.realmiracles.org/wordless-books.html

TIMES

Sometimes culturally diverse societies have a commonality of access. For example, the Internet. As oppressive countries like Iran, China, North Korea and Islamic nations find that Internet access is NOT optional if they want to do business in the global market, they have begun bringing the Internet into their geopolitical borders. Countries like China try to control free speech and thought on the Internet but that's like trying to hide sugar from ants.

Dictators who have tried to control the dissemination of information via the Internet have NOT developed an effective counter measure—and are NOT likely to do so. There are too many smart kids who can drive the "bad guys" crazier! Check out Cyber Warfare and hacking at www.uofe.org/nbc---biowarfare.html.

The technology gap between keeping the Internet out of an oppressive regime and that regime surviving well in the global market is fast closing.

Check this out. The Internet is ridiculed for its ability to quickly disseminate a "lie"—consider all the Spam hoax emails you've received. As helplessly as we try to eliminate Spam, so oppressive governments will NOT be able to "filter" out the TRUTH! Another PERFECT segment of society to reach with the message of the CROSS and God's love … and then train to reach the world in these days before the return of Messiah. Think about it—and I suggest: ACT EXPEDITIOUSLY!

SUGGESTIONS TO ADD TO YOUR GAME

1. SEND EMAIL TO GOVERNMENT, TRADE, AND UNIVERSITY OFFICES ALL OVER THE WORLD TELLING THEM ABOUT THE WEBSITE AT WWW.UOFE.ORG

FOR EMAIL ADDRESSES, LOOK IN TRADE JOURNALS, MAGAZINES, OR NEWSPAPERS. THE INTERNET IS ALSO A GOOD SOURCE. YOU MAY RECEIVE EMAIL ADDRESSES THAT ARE SENT TO YOUR WORK OR HOME, ALSO, THAT YOU MAY REPLY TO. NOBODY IS GOING TO BITE YOU. PLUS, YOU DON'T KNOW WHO IS GOING TO READ THE EMAIL ON THE OTHER END: IT MAY BE A SECRETARY—OR THE OWNER OF A BUSINESS—WHO IS READY TO COMMIT SUICIDE OR GIVE UP ON LIFE. IT MAY ALSO BE THE NEXT GREAT END TIME PROPHET! USE YOUR FAITH. ***DON'T BE AFRAID TO "COLOR OUTSIDE THE LINES!"***

SUGGESTION:
SEARCH FOR EMAIL ADDRESSES OF COMPANIES
WHICH ARE BASED INSIDE ISRAEL.

MAKE THE EMAIL MESSAGE—OR, THE REPLY—SHORT. YOU MAY WANT TO USE **YOUR OWN WEBSITE ADDRESS**; HOWEVER, **WE HAVE INCLUDED THE SITES AND EMAILS IN THESE 7 EXAMPLES IN CASE YOU DO NOT HAVE ONE.**

2. IF YOU DO A SUBSEQUENT EMAIL TO AREAS WHERE THERE MAY BE A CHRISTIAN ELEMENT THEN TELL THEM ABOUT "THE APOSTLES NEWSLETTER." THEY MAY SUBSCRIBE HERE: PRINCEHANDLEY@GMAIL.COM

3. OF COURSE, DON'T DO ANYTHING ILLEGAL, AND FOR SURE DON'T SEND "SPAM MAIL."

4. YOU SHOULD ALWAYS GIVE RECIPIENTS AN OPPORTUNITY TO "OPT OUT" AT THE END OF THE EMAIL BY PROVIDING THEM AN "UNSUBSCRIBE" EMAIL ADDRESS, EVEN IF YOU'RE ONLY SENDING THE EMAIL ONE TIME.

5. HERE ARE THREE (3) EXAMPLES OF SHORT, BUT EFFECTIVE EMAILS:

>>> MIRACLES, HEALING, PRAYER, AND HELP FOR YOU: WWW.HEALING.LIBSYN.COM

>>> STRATEGIES FOR LIVING IN THE LAST DAYS: WWW.UOFE.ORG

7. TAKE ADVANTAGE OF SOCIAL MEDIA: MYSPACE, YOUTUBE, FACEBOOK, LINKEDIN, TWITTER AND OTHERS. DIRECT THEM TO: WWW.TWITTER.COM/PRINCEHANDLEY

WHAT NOT TO DO ON SOCIAL MEDIA

Following are some "tips" gleaned from Randi Zuckerberg (sister of Facebook founder, Mark Zuckerberg) that she shared at *ClickZ Live New York* about **what NOT to do on social media**.

Vague posts

Humble bragger

Don't be a #hash #hole

Obsessive food blogger

Over-filtered Instagrammer

Romantic public exchanges

The old person who just doesn't get it

NOTE: Growing your brand with **great (helpful) content** is the number one most valuable thing you can do for your followers.

NEW TRENDS

Cars are a growing internet enabled "device" that will get a lot more development in the coming years. My new model has three (3) charging devices. (My 1991 Camaro convertible that I bought NEW has none. What does that tell you!?) **HINT: Use some audio for safe driving!**

Also, wearable internet devices are becoming—and will become—more fashionable. So, plan and implement with these new trends in mind.

If you have an IDEA or an APP that you need help developing, here are some resources for you. *Custom Made* is a community that can connect **your idea** with people that can make it happen. Creating an app is like being a maker. *App Builder* is a tool to make it easy to create **your app**. (These two hints were worth the price of the book!)

Images are proven to be more effective and inspire significantly greater engagement on social content. **Getty has released 35 million images for FREE**. Why not promote not only your posts—but also your followers from time to time—with images and photos. The new *Samsung Galaxy* smart phone has boss photo effects as well as video enhancements. So does the iPhone.

SUGGESTIONS:

1. Think of ways to make it easier for people to do what they want to while learning about Jesus.

2. Do a "digital" Sabbath one day a week. Cut yourself loose from devices, TV, computers ... even phones.

TONGUES

For creativity, power, wisdom and direction pray in the Spirit. The Holy Spirit knows HOW to reach the cultures and micro cultures. He is their Creator! Also, the Spirit of God will anoint your projects. The Bible tells us, *"Not by power nor by might, but by my Spirit says the Lord."*

The Baptism in the Holy Spirit may provide a person with a **special spirit of ability or talent**, such as:

- A spirit of craftsmanship;

- A spirit of music;

- A spirit of art;

- A spirit of creativity.

In Exodus 31, verses 1-11, a man named Bezaleel was filled with the Spirit of God in wisdom, and in understanding, and in knowledge and in all manner of workmanship. He was enabled by the Spirit to work in gold, silver, and brass; in cutting and setting stones, and in carving wood: to help in the building of the tabernacle. Another example—about 500 years later, King David said that the pattern of the temple which his son, Solomon, built was **given to David "by the Spirit."** *"All* *this,"* said David, *"the Lord made me understand in writing by his hand upon me, even all the works of this pattern."* [I Chronicles 28:12-19]

Many times you will also need protection as you work on projects the LORD assigns you.

I knew of a high school teacher who was a wonderful witness for the Jesus Christ. One day a group of students who were Satanists or witches had a curse placed on a recording. They called the teacher on his telephone to play the recording to him. Before the teacher answered the phone, the Spirit impressed him to speak in tongues when he answered the phone. **The teacher obeyed the Holy Spirit—spoke in tongues—and the recording device (the player) on the other end of the line blew up (exploded).** The next day at school this group of students told him they wanted what he had (about 10 of them as I remember) and he prayed with them to receive Christ!

In a school of ministry where I was Dean, the host pastor related a story of a Christian girl who was abducted by a group of young men. They took her in a car with the intent of raping her. The girl was a Christian, from a Christian home. Her parents were Spirit-filled; however, she had never received the Baptism of the Holy Spirit. Suddenly she decided it might help if she had this Power. She prayed to be baptized in the Spirit. **When the Holy Spirit came upon her, she spoke in**

114

tongues. The young men let her out of the car unharmed.

I prayed for an aunt of mine who was in the hospital more than 1,000 miles away. I had not seen her in years. I did NOT know what was wrong with her; only that the Lord told me to call her and pray for her in tongues. I did NOT know but she had an abdominal cancer as big as a person's fist and was to have surgery the next day. **When I prayed for her in tongues—the language of the Spirit—the cancer dissolved (disappeared) and she was healed instantly and did NOT have to have the surgery. Praise God!**

A good friend of mine, John Garlock, was raised as an MK (missionary kid) in Africa. His father, H. B. Garlock was a tremendous man of God and wrote a book named *Before They Kill and Eat You*. You may special order it at any most Christian book stores or from CFNI (Christ for the Nations Institute) in Dallas, Texas USA. Deep in the interior of a jungle region he encountered a tribe who had tied a native to a stake or tree and was **preparing to burn him alive**.

The elder Garlock attempted to intercede for the man, pleading with the tribal leaders to let the man go and have mercy on him. His plans failed and they **then tied up Garlock next to the native, preparing to burn them both**. Garlock prayed and began to speak in tongues—the language of the Spirit. Whatever the Holy

Spirit uttered through him so scared the attackers that they ran away and left the men unharmed.

The Holy Spirit will also **guide you** as well as anoint you for creativity, power and wisdom. Jesus said, *"He [The Comforter] will guide you into all truth"* ... AND ... *"He will show you things to come."* **The Spirit will not only guide you into spiritual and scriptural truth—especially the knowledge of salvation in Jesus the Messiah—but He will guide you into truth and protect you from deception in earthly matters if you seek Him and wait on Him**. He will show you things to come—not only in spiritual and scriptural issues—but also in your life ... many times warning you ahead of time of impending danger or an unwise move if you seek Him and wait on Him.

The Apostle Paul received a prophecy NOT to go up to Jerusalem, but He did because the Spirit led him to go. Another time he attempted to go into areas but he was constrained by the Spirit to NOT enter ... until the Spirit directed him to another place where God wanted him. **Let God's Spirit guide you in the projects and fields of labor where HE wants you.** He knows what is BEST for you and the people to which you are to minister!

SUMMARY

There are different **TRENDS** throughout the years and throughout your lifetime and ministry. There are different **TIMES** of refreshing as well as seasons of opportunity.

There are different ministries as well as gifts of the Holy Spirit—but only **ONE LORD**. Appropriate what He has made available to you—pray in **TONGUES** for direction—and never forget to communicate the **MESSAGE of the CROSS** which is the **POWER** of God unto salvation!

You can reach LOTS of people for Christ with the knowledge in these two books: *New Global Strategy* and *The Art of Christian Warfare*. *The Art of Christian Warfare* is a companion book to *New Global Strategy.* It is much more focused on church planting and building disciples—and also includes "tips and suggestions" for the Christian worker: on and off the field.

NOTE 1: *New Global Strategy* is ONLY available in e-Book format because there are LOTS of links (probably weeks of study in it) to help train the Christian mission director or worker. (Less pages - 37 - but lots of links).

NOTE 2: *The Art of Christian Warfare* is a manual and guide for global missions: it will get the job finished. **See the contents**. This book has the LARGEST amount of **free** pages view (for a book of this size) of any book I have ever seen on Amazon. It is 95 pages and available in both e-Book and Print format.

P.S. – We did a perusal of the available books on "Missions" online and they are generally too long AND too expensive.

Watch and pray … that you may be counted worthy to stand before the Son of Man (Yeshua) and to escape the things that are coming upon the earth. Above all, if you do NOT know the Messiah, PRAY and ask Him into your life as your LORD; ask Him to direct you and fill you with His Holy Spirit.

Pray this prayer:

> *"God of Abraham, Isaac and Jacob, if Yeshua (Jesus) is really my Messiah, reveal Him to me and I will serve you. Amen!"*

"Call to me and I will answer you, and show you great and mighty things which you do not know."
– Tanakh: Jeremiah 33:3

CREATION OF THE HEAVENS AND EARTH

Even in the most advanced area of **quantum physics** today, it is known that **the universe at its core is some sort of relationship of energy that we can NOT control.**

All processes in the universe are basically **energy conversion.**

In the area of quantum physics, time and relationship are of primal importance.

The perspective from which—or, in which—we look at things makes a big difference in our world view—and our universe view—and ultimately in our eternal view.

God could have created the heavens and the Planet Earth in six nanoseconds if He had wanted to. There was a reason he chose six literal 24-hour days to do so.

This chapter will explain HOW we can know—*and WHY we should know*—the Bible account of Creation is true.

Also, scientific fact will be presented to prove why evolution could NOT be the answer for creation; this should help build your faith in a **literal interpretation of the Creation account in Genesis Chapter One.**

For the purpose of disclosure, let me assert that I am a graduate engineer. I received my B.S. in Industrial

Engineering before attending 11 other colleges and universities. At the first institution I was the only student to ever receive a grade of 100 for the semester in the field of Electro Chemistry (which is by no means an easy subject—it is NOT even taught at many schools of higher learning). During one of the different psychology classes I have taken my I.Q. was ascertained to be 165, which is well above the floor of genius level.

I am by no means brilliant, but I do understand certain laws of physics and science, and have worked in those areas, writing my thesis in a chemical laboratory, and working consistently in research and development using instruments such as the Atom Counter as well as the usual instrumentation for determining qualitative and quantitative analyses.

My views are based—not from the standpoint of one who believes the Bible is the Word of God, although I do—but from the standpoint of one who has studied and worked in the fields of science and engineering. As an engineer I could no more believe in the theory of evolution than the cow jumping over the moon. Not only is there **NO evidence that evolution has ever taken place**, but there is **solid evidence that evolution could NEVER take place**.

Evolution could not even be possible because it violates both the First and Second Law of Thermodynamics. I will explain below.

SECOND LAW OF THERMODYNAMICS

The Second Law of Thermodynamics is also known as the **Entropy Principle**, which is one of the most universal and fixed laws known to science. *"There is a general natural tendency of all observed systems to go from order to disorder, reflecting dissipation of energy available for future transformation—the law of increasing entropy."*

All processes in the universe are basically **energy conversion**. Thermodynamics is a compound of two Greek words, **therme** ("heat") and **dunamis** ("power"). It is the science of heat energy (or, heat power) and its conversion to other forms of energy. **Everything that exists in the universe is some form of energy, and everything that happens is a type or form of energy conversion**. With this in mind, let us discuss the First Law of Thermodynamics.

FIRST LAW OF THERMODYNAMICS

One of the best definitions for the First Law is from Isaac Asimov: *"In the Game of Energy and Thermodynamics You Can't Break Even,"*

Smithsonian Institute Journal:

> *"Energy can be transferred from one place to another, or transformed from one form to another, but it [energy] can be neither created nor destroyed. Or, we can put it another way: The*

*total quantity of energy in the universe is **constant.** **When the total quantity of something does not change, we say that it is conserved.** The two statements given above, then, are two ways of expressing **'the law of conservation of energy.'** This law is considered the most powerful and most fundamental generalization about the universe that scientists have ever been able to make."*

Before we go on, let's consider something Asimov said. *"Energy ... can be neither created nor destroyed."* **Energy can NOT be created because God is the only One Who can create energy and He ceased creative process in the universe after the first six days.** That is the purpose for the Sabbath: to rest from our labor, to receive BLESSING from God, and to reflect on the creative glory and goodness of God. (Torah: Genesis 2:3) On the other hand, energy can NOT be destroyed because God upholds all things in creation by the Word of His power (Hebrews 1:3).

In the area of quantum physics, time and relationship are of primal importance. Many theories relating to time have been developed over the years. Probably the most famous is that developed by Albert Einstein: the theory of relativity.

I read his work as a young boy. The derived formula "**E = mc^2**," or "energy equals mass times the velocity of light squared," was praised for decades as the frontier of thought in this area; however, recent scientific postulation and research has leaned toward discrediting part, if not all, of this theory.

The universe at its core is some sort of relationship of energy that we can NOT control.

Even in the most advanced area of **quantum physics** today, it is known that **the universe at its core is some sort of relationship of energy that we can NOT control**. In the area of string theory today, the comparison picture (relational size and properties) is this: the universe is to the earth, as the earth is to an atom, as an atom is to a "string" (that is, a "string" in string theory).

–The issue is not *the big-ness or the out-ness ...* or *the small-ness or the in-ness* ... but **the real issue is multiple dimensions of reality**. In other words, not "either - or" but "yes – and." String theorists now say they can prove eleven (11) dimensions of reality, and maybe 12 or 13.

The perspective from which—or, in which—we look at things makes a big difference in our world view—and our universe view—and ultimately in our eternal view. If we look at things in a dream world, as the evolutionist does (even in our human three-dimensional perspective), where there is NO sustainable evidence—from the past or present—we are saying willingly in our heart (and NOT our mind) *"There is NO God."* At least, NOT the Creator God. *"The fool has said in his heart, 'There is NO God.'"* (Psalm 14:1)

The present underpinning of the universe is conservation of energy, not creation. No creation in the universe has taken place since the first six days. The evolutionist has NO valid answer to the following questions:

- Where did all the energy come from in the first place (Who started everything); and,

- Why is energy constant (being conserved)?

The First Law of Thermodynamics is a strong scientific testimony against evolution because it proves **constancy** and stability in the universe. However, the Second Law of Thermodynamics is even more potent in that it completely obliterates any rationale for evolutionary thinking. R.B. Lindsay, in his article in **American Scientist**, titled, *"Entropy Consumption and Values in Physical Science,"* states:

> *"It is in the transformation process that **Nature appears to exact a penalty** and this is where the second principle makes its appearance. For every naturally occurring transformation of energy is*

*accompanied, somewhere, **by a loss in the availability of energy for the future performance of work.***"

In any energy conversion there is an amount of energy which becomes UNavailable for subsequent processes or work. It will be nonrecoverable. The late Henry Morris, PhD., states this succinctly:

*"Thus, **the Second Law proves, as certainly as science can prove anything whatever, that the universe had a beginning. Similarly, the First Law shows that the universe could not have begun itself.** The **total quantity of energy in the universe is** a **constant, but** the quantity of **AVAILABLE energy is decreasing.***

IMPORTANT

*Therefore, as we go backward in time, the available energy would have been progressively greater until, finally, we would **reach the beginning point, where available energy equaled total energy.** Time could go back no further than this. **At this point both energy and time must have come into existence.** Since energy could not create itself, the most scientific and logical conclusion to which we could possibly come is that: 'In the beginning, God created the heaven and the earth.'"*

125

Isaac Asimov stated, *"The universe is constantly getting more disorderly."* All real processes—chemical, physical, biological, geological—go from order to disorder: the exact opposite of evolutionary theory.

When something is new (whether it be a life form or a manufactured object) it takes on the condition of a **closed state**. A baby formed in the life of its mother, when it exits the womb, is an example of this: it grows older and eventually dies. A new building is another example: through time, corrosion, decay, weathering, and stress take their toll. Everything deteriorates by itself. There are NO observable processes of development from a lower order to a higher order or from disorder to order.

In six literal 24 hour days, the LORD God made the heavens and the Planet Earth. **God is God. He did NOT need the help of so called evolutionary processes—millions or billions of years between each Day of Creation—to help Him create.** God could have created the heavens and the Planet Earth in six nanoseconds if He had wanted to. He gave us a practical and orderly example **that we could relate to**: work six days and rest one.

NOTICE

That creation is **exactly that time period** is verified in the *Ten Commandments* (Torah: Exodus Chapter 20):

"Remember the Sabbath day to keep it holy.

Six days shall you labor, and do all your work:

But the seventh day is the Sabbath of the LORD your God;

In it you shall not do any work, you, nor your son, nor your daughter, your manservant, nor your maidservant, nor your cattle, nor the stranger that is within your gates;

For in six days the LORD made heaven and earth, *the sea, and all that in them is, and* **rested the seventh day***:*

Wherefore the LORD blessed the Sabbath day, and made it holy."

Messiah Yeshua validated the CREATION account in the Torah, referring to Genesis: [1] *"But from the beginning of the creation God made them male and female;"* and by his statement, [2] *"The sabbath was made for man, and not man for the sabbath: Therefore the Son of man is Lord also of the sabbath."* (Brit Chadashah: Mark 10:6, Matthew 19:4-6, Mark 2:27)

The main reason that many people who claim to know the LORD and who are conservative or orthodox Jews, or conservative or orthodox Christians, swing toward evolutionary creationism is because **they are ashamed to take a stand for a literal six day 24 hour day**

creation week. They feel they will be laughed at by friends, colleagues, and others. They are **bowing** at the throne of Darwin and the throne of political correctness which is very dangerous. **Can you claim to be a follower of The Messiah but NOT believe in a literal interpretation of the very Creation account that Yeshua validated?!**

I trust this teaching has helped you.

NOTHING CAN BIND YOU

Have you ever had a time when you were struggling between two choices—two alternative decisions you could make? But ... you made a bad decision. Afterwards you felt sick in your spirit—you felt like glue!

There is absolutely NO situation in your life that can bind you if you will follow your heart as God leads you. This chapter will teach you how to get out of any situation that has you bound. Even if the situation was a result of a bad decision, a mistake—or, sin.

You have spiritual desires and you have material desires. But remember—**your enemy, the devil, does NOT want you to have any of your good desires! He wants YOU bound! But ... Jesus wants you FREE.**

This section will provide you with simple—but effective—steps for your escape to FREEDOM, BLESSING, SUCCESS and POWER.

Nothing can bind you!

There is absolutely NO situation in your life that can bind you if you will follow your heart as God leads you.

LET ME REPEAT: There is absolutely NO situation in your life that can bind you if you will follow your heart as God leads you.

God not only wants to meet your NEEDS, but He wants to give you the DESIRES of your heart. *"Delight yourself also in the Lord, and He shall give you the desires of your heart."* [Psalm 37:4]

The Hebrew word for "**delight**" in this passage means, "**have pleasurable emotion.**" In other words, **ENJOY Jesus**! Whether through praise, dancing, prayer, works, singing in tongues, fellowship—delight yourself in Him—and He will give you the [good] desires of your heart.

God GIVES you the desires of your heart in a two-fold manner, like an engine and a caboose on a train:

By **allowing** the desires in your heart as you walk with Him;

By **granting** the desires after you walk in obedience to Him.

Notice the time factor: between the "engine" and the "caboose." There is a segment of time (sometimes almost instantaneous), but more usually an elapsed time of days, years, or maybe decades.

You have SPIRITUAL desires: to be used by God, for the gifts of the Holy Spirit to operate through you, or to be a blessing to people and nations. **You also have material desires**: for a house, car, furniture, food, and clothing.

Remember ... **the enemy, the devil, does NOT want you to have any of your good desires!** He will tell you, *"God doesn't want to use you; that's just your imagination."* **But he is lying to you**. Hang on to that vision!

The Bible tells us in Romans 2:28-29, *"For he is not a Jew who is one outwardly, nor is circumcision that which is outward in the flesh; but he is a Jew who is one inwardly; and circumcision is that of the heart, in the Spirit, not in the letter; whose praise*** is not from men but from God."*

*** Notice that the word "**praise**" here is a play on words. "praise" is literally "Jew". Whose praise (hou ho epainos). The antecedent of the relative hou is Ioudaios (Jew). Probably a reference to the etymology of Judah (praise) as seen in Genesis 49:8 in the Torah.

There is a place in man where God has a spiritual center: it is the "heart" ... or the "spirit" of man. Ezekiel prophesied to the house of Israel that in the last days, *"[God] will take you from among the nations, gather you out of all countries, and bring you into your own land." "I* *will give you a new heart, and put a new spirit within you."* [Ezekiel 36:24, 26]

"Therefore, if any man is IN Christ, he is a NEW creation; old things have passed away, behold all things have become new." [2 Corinthians 5:17]

The Apostle Peter wrote about *"the hidden person of the heart."* [1 Peter 3:4]

God not only gives you the desires of your heart, but **He will LEAD YOU by your heart if you are following Him, living for Him.** But if you're not following God, don't follow your heart. *"The spirit of man is the lamp of the Lord, searching all the inner depths of the heart."* [Proverbs 20:27]

Have you ever had a time when you were struggling between two choices—two alternative decisions you could make? But ... you made a bad decision. Afterwards you felt sick in your spirit—you felt like glue! You DID NOT LISTEN to your hidden (inner man) ... the spirit man of your heart. *"For as many are led by the Spirit of God, these are the sons of God."*

Even a person who is not a Christian can know things in his human spirit. Man is a spirit being made in the image of God. However, if a person who is NOT living for God makes a BAD decision there is no guarantee he can be free. He may pay for his bad choice the rest of his life.

But the person **who lives for Christ** has spiritual power so that **he or she can become FREE**; he or she does not have to be bound by that bad choice. **There is a way out!**

I ministered with a friend who was an attorney and had been sent to prison for life. While he was serving his life sentence in a Federal Prison (USA) he became a Christian. One day not announced to him—and completely unexpected—guards came to him and escorted him to an area where he was released. He then became a minister.

Sometimes we make bad decisions—mistakes—or choices. When this happens **there are four (4) things you can do for your deliverance:**

Pray and ask God to smite Satan (even through the bad decision) and turn the situation around for God's glory.

Ask God for a MIRACLE. Give God a gift offering (it may be your time, service, or money) ahead of time as "faith–thanks" for turning the situation around.

Find a promise or promises in God's Word that pertain to the situation and lean on them: speak them out regularly in your fellowship with the Lord.

Take authority over Satan in the name of Jesus, the Messiah, and "break" the power of the bad decision.

Speak and command the power of the bad decision or choice to be broken in the name of Jesus Christ, God's Son and Messiah!

There is NO situation in life that can bind you if you will surrender to Christ and follow your heart as God leads you!

Enjoy your freedom. Go help others!

P.S.– Study the book *Action Keys for Success*. Learn KEY steps to enter the vortex of the anointing so that you can be on the "cutting edge" to help you **create and maintain new exploits** for the LORD and for yourself.

ANOINTED SLOWDOWN FOR YOUR MIRACLE

We know that certain situations must come to pass in the Last Days. However, our job is to be an influence in the generation and environment in which God has placed us.

We are to be Soldiers of the Spirit—Prophets of Pentecost. To help in this great End Time—God anointed—conscription of **people called to the prophetic service**, I have provided specific—but simple—instructions for a **productive, peaceful and powerfully anointed lifestyle**.

Also, included in this chapter is a **PROPHECY** concerning the next great spiritual awakening ... plus a **WARNING** about economic conditions.

Slow down. Don't load your plate—or your palate—with too much! **Focus and stay free!**

This chapter will show you HOW to slow down and receive POWER and REFRESHING—plus what steps to take in order to call into being prophetic MIRACLES: for NOW and for the FUTURE.

Tough times are coming and **your strength is to wait on God**.

*"Therefore the Lord will **wait**, that He may be gracious to you; And therefore He will be exalted, that He may have mercy **on** you. For the Lord is a **God** of justice; Blessed are all those who **wait** for Him."* (Isaiah 30:18)

Things look good sometimes and bad other times—*if you're focused on the stock market and employment*—as far as the economy is concerned; however, "What you see is NOT always what you get" in natural sight.

**Tough times are coming and
your strength is to wait on God**.

Economic conditions NOW are NOT precursors for conditions FUTURE. What is coming will be WORSE than 2001 and 2008. Make sure—if you live in a metroplex—that you are prayed up and protected.

If you follow my BLOG you will know that in 2008 I told my subscribers to **SELL** any real estate that was not their primary residence (unless, of course, they needed it for business). And, I told them to **BUY** real estate again in 2012 and 2013 when real estate was on the upswing. I followed my own instructions—4 months early in September, 2011—by the leading of the LORD. Check a graph of real estate values and you will see this advice was "spot on."

Your greatest investment to protect you and protect your family from the coming downturn is sowing into God's Work.

START NOW!!!

However, I have GREAT NEWS for you. **What you SEE—what you envision—with your mind's eye in FAITH is what you get**.

I have a prophetic message for YOU from God.

- Slow down NOW.

- Get involved helping others

- Do NOT overload yourself with schedule.

- Cut out in your mind's eye what you want in the future.

- Write down your Spirit goals and claim Mark 11:24 regularly.

SLOW DOWN NOW

The reason you need to slow down NOW is because stressful times are coming. You will need all the "preparation" you can get to maintain spiritual equilibrium

I have developed two different definitions of "spiritual balance" over the years. I used to get so tired of hearing theologians and Bible teachers using the term "balanced" as an excuse for NOT evangelizing vigorously, NOT being bold in the faith or NOT making waves. So I taught people in my seminars that being "balanced" spiritually is "to be radical in every direction." My other definition of "balance"—the micro one—is to maintain a "peace zone" out of which you refuse to wander. That is, **stay in Area 14 where you refuse to be bothered: by Satan, by demons, by people … even by Christians**.

I just experienced an incident with a friend—who I thought was close, but who was definitely agitated by Satan over waters long past—while I was planning one of the most strategic projects for Jews in Israel. In those times, especially when you are involved in strategic planning for the LORD, **do NOT embrace that spirit of discord. Let it go! You have better roads to travel**. Also, **situations when people (or, demons) come "out of the woodwork" can be great "signs" for you that what you are working on is SUPER important for the LORD** … and for the people you're going to reach. You can smile—sit back—and laugh at the devil. **Focus and stay free!**

GET INVOLVED HELPING OTHERS

Select a way to help others: a ministry by which you can serve God.

You already may be involved in ministry of some sort, but spend more time helping individuals "one-on-one." This can be in addition to what you are already doing. However, re-arrange your schedule to give you "flex-time." **Make sure you allow for more "breathing space.**" REST!!!

"In returning and rest you will be saved (made whole). In quietness and in confidence will be your victory." – Isaiah 30:15

I received a MIRACLE healing through the above Scripture one time. I had been so busy serving God that I had NOT been observing my Sabbath Rest. (*Sometimes if I have been ministering on Sundays, I rest on Mondays.*) I was in an Isolation Ward with several rare diseases. Not even the nurse could come into the room. The nurse had to take my information from outside the room. She asked me: *"What is your date of birth?"* I said, *"Which one do you want?"* She said, *"Do you mean you have had MORE than one birth?"* I said, *"Yes. When I was born naturally from my mother ... and when I was born supernaturally by the Holy Spirit of God when I received Jesus Christ as my Lord."* The nurse answered and said, *"I know what you're saying is true. My father is a minister but I have never experienced it."*

You have to take your Day of Rest that God provided to refresh you. **During that day I often declare prophetically into nations and groups—and myself—for great works of God.** And those prophetic declarations include WAYS and MEANS of helping people: now and in the future.

Sometimes—especially at the end of the day—I do NOT feel like ministering to people. However, I then think of HOW the LORD did NOT feel like going to the cross—*and staying on the cross*—for me! So, I continue. Sometimes it may be replying to email requests for prayer, or calling a person on the phone who needs help. I never have the problem when ministering to a crowd because there is a special anointing in those environments. But ... Jesus died for individuals. Never stop helping people "one-on-one." **But maintain your rest so you can stay free!**

DO NOT OVERLOAD YOURSELF

You need to learn when to say, "No." If you wear yourself down you will NOT be able to minister effectively to others. Set a schedule and stick with it. Lots of ministers have died from heart attacks. They went home prematurely and cut off people from their ministry.

Learn to establish boundaries of time, relationships and money. Do NOT put undue pressure on yourself. **You are the master of your time**. You are NOT a slave to a schedule. **There is ENOUGH time to do what God wants you to do!** The One Who is the Beginning and the End, the Alpha and the Omega, has given you ENOUGH TIME to do what He wants you to do. Your job is to find out—to determine—**WHAT** He wants you to do. This is arrived at by spending daily time in Bible reading, prayer, meditation, and from time-to-time fasting.

- Know WHAT you want to do (that is, what God wants you to do); and,

- Plan HOW to do it.

You also need to determine how to profit from your leisure, or non-work, time. Is watching TV a profitable experience for you? Sometime it is: if you are relaxing, or learning, or being inspired. But the next day ask yourself, *"In what way did I profit from watching TV yesterday?"* If you determine that you did not profit from that experience, then change your life style. Spend your non-work time creating, praying, building your mind, body, and spirit; also, listening and playing.

Also, do NOT put off plans or experiences because of TIME. Jump in! If God wants you to do it, then take the TIME. **God will make a way for you to do what He wants you to do, but YOU have to INITIATE the action with FAITH.**

CUT OUT IN YOUR MIND'S EYE

While at a large metropolitan city—I don't remember where—I was in a hotel room reflecting, praying, and meditating before going to minister. Several stories up, I was looking out over the city to a large forest. I thought, **"Where did all those trees come from?"** As quickly as I had this thought, came an answer: **"From a seed."**

What kind of forest would you like—or need—to grow today? Is it a forest for your family, for your ministry, for the nations of the world ... or for something personal in your life?

This is where the POINT OF DECISION is so important. **Learn to ACT towards God at the point of decision.** My mother used to say, *"You should have nipped it in the bud."* We are continuously growing forests: either negatively or positively. This is why Jesus said: *"For a beautiful tree does not produce worthless fruit; neither does a rotten tree produce valuable fruit."* (Luke 6:43)

In the book of Job—Chapter 22, verse 28—we read an amazing truth: *"You will also decree a thing, and it shall be established unto you ..."* In the original Hebrew language the word "decree" is a primitive root form of the word "gazar," which means **"to cut out exclusively, or to decide."** In its primitive form it is used also as a "quarrying" term ... as in cutting out stone from a rock quarry. It means more than to "say" or "speak." **It**

conveys the meaning of "cutting something out in your mind's eye" ... that is, "to envision—to make a vision—**to decide upon it**, and confess it" ... and then it will be established unto you!

Learn to spend quality time meditating and thinking—visualizing in the mind's eye of your heart—the GREAT THINGS you want to do for God. Plant and grow GIANT FORESTS of good. Remember, God promised you that He is *"able to do exceeding abundantly above all that you ask or think."* (Ephesians 3:20) Spend time planting and cultivating your forest. Any worthwhile thing in life takes time, so why not spend good quality time planning and preparing your forest: **Cut it out in your mind's eye. Then, decree prophetically and bring it into existence.**

WRITE DOWN YOUR SPIRIT GOALS

Write down you Spirit directed goals so you can meditate upon them—pray about them—and receive them by FAITH. Decree their implementation prophetically! Once you SEE it you can bring it to pass prophetically by FAITH. Many people have been helped by my book, *Faith and Quantum Physics.* It has helped them to know the reality of God's universal laws and how faith decrees—working with God's laws—can bring into reality things that previously were only possibilities and probabilities.

By writing down your Spirit directed goals—those goals you have obtained by the leading of God through prayer, vision and faith—you have **record of the evidence** upon which to target your faith. I keep mine on a 3 x 5 index card where they are easy to keep with me in a shirt pocket, Bible or notebook. Nations are in the balance. People and ethnic groups are needing deliverance and MIRACLES. You can also write down or memorize Scriptures that pertain to each of your Holy Spirit defined goals. Or, if you need scripture affirmations pertaining to the **Four Pillars of Life for YOU**, then you will find them in my book, *Total Person Toolbox*. Stay powerful, whole, prosperous and authoritative with this book.

Also, learn to use a "catalyst" with your prophetic decrees by receiving them in FAITH via Messiah Jesus' promise in Mark 11:24: *"Whatever things you ask for* **when you pray, believe that you receive them,** *and you will have them."*

Many people will be used by the LORD in these End Times through the ministry of creative prophecy. Prophetic decrees established in the Spirit and carried out by the prophet will bring MIRACLE happenings to many sectors of society.

- Politicians, government leaders and evil dictators will be removed from office.

- Confusion will be loosed into evil empires and groups like ISIS with many being saved.

- Great spiritual awakenings will happen with MIRACLES in public places.

- Many in the cults, occult and false religions will be visited by Messiah Jesus.

We know that certain situations must come to pass in the Last Days. However, our job is to be an influence in the generation and environment in which God has placed us. We are to be Soldiers of the Spirit—Prophets of Pentecost. To help in this great End Time—God anointed—conscription of people called to the Office of Prophet, I have written the book, *Prophecy, Transition & Miracles*. If you feel that the LORD is calling you for this purpose in this day and hour, then everything you need for instruction is in this book. It will jump start YOU.

Now ... go enjoy your life's work and WIN!

DEALING WITH STRESS: HEALTH AND PREVENTION

> **"But know this, that in the last days**
> **perilous times will come."**
> 2 Timothy 3:1-5

Because of "barrenness of virtue" there is—*and will be in the future*—much corruption in commerce, in government and in personal relationships—*not to mention the economic landscape*—resulting in hard, painful and stressful conditions in the lives of people.

This chapter will teach you how to PREVENT stress from operating in your life. Instead of "fixing" the situation, you will learn some areas of preventive maintenance to **avoid** stress in your life.

The reader will learn four (4) symptoms of stress, four (4) areas of attack against you ... and four (4) KEYS to prevention, healing and health.

This section is an excellent resource—not only for your life, family and work—but for you to share with others who need help!

This is truly a mini power chapter for not only dealing with—*but preventing*—stress!

"But know this, that in the last days perilous times will come."
2 Timothy 3:1-5

The Greek word for "perilous" used in the passage above is the word "chalepos" (khal-ep-**oss**) and means: **"harsh, fierce, difficult, dangerous, painful, grievous, hard to deal with."**

It describes a society that has replaced virtue with immorality: and this **includes governments and leaders in government**. In addition, the void left by deleting virtue invites the entrance of demonic spirits to operate within the arts, the media, commerce, and governmental and legal structures of society.

In this chapter I want to help you learn **How to Protect Yourself from Stress**. I want to teach you how to PREVENT stress from operating in your life. Instead of "fixing" the situation, I want to teach you some areas of preventive maintenance to **avoid** stress in your life.

After I received the Mikvah of Ruach HaKodesh (the Baptism in the Holy Spirit) I did lots of research on fasting and health. I noticed that in the Scandinavian countries there was more emphasis of fasting than in the West. Some Scandinavians would fast one day a week or three days a month. Also, their medical practice was based more on a **preventive regimen** than on "fix it after the problem."

I have a very honest auto mechanic that has worked on my automobiles for 30 years. Sometimes he does not even charge me. Other times, he will say, *"You don't need that."* And many times he has told me things that I should do to prevent mechanical failures, whereas, he could have NOT mentioned these things and waited until something broke and then charged me.

I want to tell you HOW to prevent stress from happening in your life: **How to Protect Yourself from Stress**. In Job 3:26 we read, *"I am not at ease, neither am I quiet, neither have I rest; But trouble comes."* Pertinent to the message in this book, I want to emphasize that Job in this situation (before he was healed) was:

- Not at ease;

- Disquieted;

- Restless; and,

- Troubled.

Proverb 27:12 tells us, *"A prudent person foresees danger and takes precautions. The simpleton goes blindly on and suffers the consequences."* I have done

148

lots of investing through the years by day trading and investing in commodities and futures where I operated with **large margins** for the advantage of leverage. Of course, if the trades went "south" the margins worked to my disadvantage. But, here, I want to illustrate the good use of margins. **The definition of "margin" is "An amount available beyond what is actually needed."** One source describes it as, "The space between our current load and our limits."

WHEN YOU DON'T HAVE MARGIN

- Stress goes up

- Focus narrows

- Relationships suffer***

- You are not prepared for the future

***Notice**: Relationships only start ... are nourished ... during margin.

In Luke 17:1, Messiah Yeshua taught: *"Things that cause people to stumble are bound to come ..."* This is where "margin" can be a buffer to protect you from stress.

HOW YOU DEVELOP MARGIN

- Slow down.

- Simplify things in your life: activities, stuff, technology.

- Allow for and establish time, money, work and relationship margins.

- Give yourself SPACE.

Don't make things too binding—too tight—too limited: **Plan for MARGIN in your time, your financial dealings, your work, your relationships!**

The **time** margin is one of the easiest to "fix," but at the same time, the one we prioritize least when planning. Messiah Jesus was asked the question: *"Rabbi, which is the greatest commandment in Torah?"* Yeshua answered, *"Love the Lord your God with all your heart and with all your soul and with all your mind."* This is the first and greatest commandment. And the second is like it: *"Love your neighbor as yourself."* All the Law and the Prophets hang on these two commandments.

LOVE provides—it leads the way—for "margin."

However, the "mechanics" of margin are maintained during Sabbath: the day of rest. The mechanics of margin such as:

- The need for it;

- The desire for it; and,

- The "how to" plans for it.

These are inculcated during the Day of Rest with God.

Also, during the Day of Rest there are TWO promised blessings shown in Isaiah Chapter 58:

- You will *"ride on the high places of the earth,"* and ...

- You will *"feed on the heritage of Jacob, your father."*

In other words, you will be:

- Above, and in control of the events in your life, with "heights" of enjoyment.

- Prosperous, healthy and fruitful.

My friend, start today establishing margins in your family, your finances and your field of endeavor.

Give yourself SPACE. Don't make things too binding—too tight—too limited: for yourself, your family and your associates. **Plan for margin!** It will protect you from stress NOW ... and in the troubling times to come.

GOD DOESN'T TELL YOU WHY: HE SHOWS YOU

I was invited to speak at several public high schools before the nationalization of Zimbabwe. In every one of the schools where I ministered the gifts of the Holy Spirit operated and God performed MIRACLES.

However, I did NOT lay hands on the students myself. When I laid my hands on a student and prayed **nothing** happened. **I asked God, "WHY?"**

I asked God two other big "WHY's" pertaining to my ministry there. But, regardless of all the "WHY's" I saw God's mighty hand at work in MIRACLES: miracles in people and in a nation.

This chapter will teach you that God does NOT have to tell you "WHY" ... He will show you!!!

He always has a reason—and if we just obey—His purpose will be carried out and become productive.

It is counter-intuitive to presuppose God. This section will build your faith to trust Him—and His purposes—when He speaks to your heart about doing something: even IF it seems foolish.

What is God asking YOU to do?

WHAT IS GOD ASKING YOU TO DO?

In 1976 the LORD told me to go to Rhodesia, which is now Zimbabwe, and preach the Good News with signs following. This, of course, included training people as Jesus commanded us in the Great Commission: instructing believers about the Baptism in the Holy Spirit with the evidence of speaking in other tongues. Many MIRACLES happened.

I believe lots of bloodshed was avoided as a result of my ministry there as it preceded the nationalization of the country. A white minority government used to control the country until 1979. Following THAT WAS a brutal guerrilla war fought with two rival African nationalist organizations (Robert Mugabe's ZANU party and Joshua Nkomo's ZAPU party). Rhodesian premier Ian Smith then conceded to biracial democracy in 1978.

A provisional government subsequently headed by Smith and his moderate colleague Abel Muzorewa failed in appeasing international critics or halting the bloodshed. Finally, the Republic of Zimbabwe was established and has remained so since 1980. The economic condition of the country has suffered terribly under its recent socialist government.

In Germany's Weimar Republic, there was a three-year period of hyperinflation between June 1921 and January 1924 where the German mark went from 4.2 marks per

U.S. dollar to 4.2 Billion marks to the dollar. This rampant inflation was one of the reasons Adolf Hitler and the Nazi party came to power in that country.

During my time in Rhodesia I was taken out into the rural areas where, at 1 to 2 AM in the dark night, I would see hordes of people marching silently, inspired by Communist leadership, preparing for socialist revolt and overthrow of the ruling party. Economic conditions seemed unfair to the mass of the populace then—but **nowhere in comparison to the terrible economic status of the country NOW and since 1979.**

Zimbabwe is a more recent example of inflation run wild. At its peak in November 2008, **inflation was running at 6.5 sextillion percent**. Zimbabwe still has no national currency; currencies from other countries are used. The economy is wrecked under socialist Mugabe but **God can break the curse of civil war**—and—any curse. Mugabe's death may bring it (he is over 92). Mugabe said, *"The only white man you can trust is a dead white man."*

The young people I trained in Rhodesia (now Zimbabwe) can be God's agents to bring an anointing from The Breaker to bring the country forward. *"With men it is impossible, but with God all things are possible." PRAY for Zimbabwe!*

While I was in Rhodesia I was invited to speak at several public schools with age brackets corresponding to high school in the USA. **In every one of the schools where I ministered the gifts of the Holy Spirit operated and God performed MIRACLES.** At the first school where I ministered I taught on *"Jesus, the Healer."* At the end of my teaching, I started to pray for students ... but nothing happened. I asked God, *"WHY? What is wrong?"*

The LORD spoke to me and said, *"I don't want you to pray for the students. I want you to teach them HOW to pray for each other. Because when you leave, they will just say, 'It was a white man from USA who came to pray for us.'"*

I did what God told me. I began having the students lay hands on each other and every one I know of who needed healing was healed. In every high school I went to after that, I did the same thing. **God would give me a Word of Knowledge about a condition in a student that I did NOT know (a condition in their body); I would call them out, and then have another student or students lay hands on them in Jesus' name and they would always be healed.** Many students received Christ as a result of witnessing the MIRACLES.

The saddest school where I went to minister was referred to as a "colored" school. The students were "mixed" from African and Caucasian backgrounds, with some from parents from India. You could feel the heaviness in the spirit of the students. They were persecuted by both blacks and by whites. But—praise God—after the Lord Jesus visited them they did NOT have that problem. The spirit of heaviness was broken and **they experienced the JOY of the LORD!**

What is God asking YOU to do?

One day while at lunch I overheard a man's name mentioned in a conversation. He was the head over ALL media in Rhodesia. His name was Val Lunn. The next day, the LORD told me to go see that man. I did NOT know where he was, nor how to find him (I had merely heard his name mentioned). **I knew that he was head of Rhodesian Broadcasting Corporation so I found out the address of that office.** I did not have access to an automobile and there was no transportation available in the area where I was staying (it was a very exclusive area).

I started walking in faith. I was comfortable with this as previously I had lived on the streets, preaching the Gospel, and used my feet to get me places for years. After walking a short distance, I heard an automobile stop beside me. A lady was driving, and she said in a very commanding voice: *"Get in, sit down!"* (I later asked God if he had any angels that looked like a lady!) She asked me where I was going. I told her the address but that I did NOT know HOW to get there. She drove me to the head office of Rhodesian Broadcasting Corporation.

When I arrived at RBC I told the receptionist that I wanted to talk to Mr. Val Lunn. She responded by telling me that he alternated offices, flying between Bulawayo and Salisbury, the capital (after 1982 it was named Harare), every other day. She said that Mr. Lunn would be back in Bulawayo where I was staying the next day. I left a note for him saying, *"I am from California, USA, and the LORD told me to come see you."*

The next day I received a phone call from Mr. Lunn inviting me to come talk with him. I went to his office and shared with him the Good News of Jesus Christ. **He told me he wanted to be saved and prayed with me, receiving Christ as His Lord. Then, I laid hands on him and he received the Baptism in the Holy Spirit and started speaking in tongues**. While he was speaking in tongues, he had his eyes closed and I left his office and walked away. He did not know I had left.

A few days later Mr. Lunn called me and asked me to come to his home and baptize him in his swimming pool. He also requested that I lead his house servant to Christ, both of which I did. After being baptized, Mr. Lunn told me this: he said, *"I want Christ to use me in the media."* Since he was head of ALL media in Rhodesia, including radio and television, I recognized it as a great open door for the nation to hear about Jesus.

When I returned to the United States I notified the top three Christian television ministries that Val Lunn wanted Christian videos and programming sent to him to air on TV. (Pat Robertson of CBN called me to ask about what God had done in Rhodesia while I was there.) **None of the top 3 Christian TV ministries ever responded to Val Lunn's request for video teaching.** I even re-contacted one or two of them, but no response. **I asked God, *"Why don't these ministries want to help?"***

Then I realized, *"God does NOT have to tell me 'WHY.'"* But I soon found out "WHY." While I had been in Rhodesia I was holding a teaching seminar with several young black nationals. These young people were brilliant (two of them were bankers and drew European wages) but they had NO money. None of them had a motor car; only one had a small cycle.

We met for the teaching sessions in an underground basement (there was NO floor above ground). There were buckets on the floor to catch rain water from ground level above. I even asked God, *"WHY don't you provide a better place for these meetings?"*

Later, the LORD showed me WHY. It was still a time of strict segregation and God wanted me to teach this special group of black young men and women He had called out. Authorities would not have allowed them—or me—in a so-called "white" facility.

Every session that I taught I was impressed by the Holy Spirit to teach them, *"Do NOT trust the God of the United States for your finances; trust the God of Elijah."* And, I taught a lot about the life of Elijah.

After I had been back in the USA for a few weeks I received a letter from the people I had been teaching in the underground seminar. (It was truly an "underground" seminar.) They said, *"We just made our first five (5) television shows!"*

Then I realized: ***"That's WHY God did NOT want the top three TV ministries in the USA to send any programming to Rhodesia."*** It was the time of nationalization. **God wanted the TV programs to be ALL BLACK programming**. I had never connected these young people with Val Lunn ... and I do NOT know whether he had sought them out ... but GOD DID IT.

There was a lot of bloodshed in the few years following, However, I believe lots of bloodshed was avoided as a result of my ministry in Rhodesia as it preceded the nationalization of the country, and many received the Good News on TV programs produced by the young Blacks I trained during this troublesome time.

By God's grace we published and distributed thousands of the *Wordless Books* in Zimbabwe. We supplied thousands to one missionary who baptized over 2,000 people and started over 800 churches there.

What is God telling YOU to do???

Remember, GOD DOES NOT HAVE TO TELL YOU WHY. Just obey Him ... and He will show you!

KNOW WHEN TO GIVE – WHEN NOT TO GIVE

Recently I had just awakened from my night's sleep and the LORD instructed me to contact a friend of mine who is a world-class athlete—and a household name in the football (soccer) world.

God impressed me to tell him the contents of this teaching so that he would not have confusion in the future regarding "**when to give and when not to give**" AND to **protect** him in the future.

I have a ministry associate who has been my personal friend for over 35 years who was really being "ripped off" by people—*ministers*—who claimed to be Christians. They were greatly taking advantage of him financially due to his kindness and Christian charity. I had counseled him different times concerning what basically is the content of this chapter. He finally "saw the light."

It is my prayer that this section will **help** YOU—and **protect** YOU—in the future. I believe I have covered all the groundwork situationally that you might experience with regards to meeting needs. I pray that with wisdom and the guidance of the Holy Spirit you may serve in optimum stewardship for the Kingdom of God … and for yourself.

True spirituality is "seeing a need and meeting it." Sometimes, you may not be able to physically meet the needs of other people. But, you can always take the people to God in prayer. Actually, that's what ministry is: "serving people by taking them to God." Our beloved brother James said, *"Suppose there are brothers or sisters who need clothes and don't have enough to eat. What good is there in your saying to them, 'God bless you! Keep warm and eat well!' if you don't give them the necessities of life? So it is with faith: if it is alone and has no actions with it, then it is dead."* (James 2:15-17)

>>> Prayer is an "action" that you can always take. It is not an excuse to keep from helping someone in a physical way. The most important thing you can always give a person is the Word of God. If you give money to a poor person, he will usually end up being poor again; however, if you give him the Gospel (all the Good News, not part of it), he will learn how to serve God and to tithe and offer to His Heavenly Father; then, God will take care of him and he will not starve in time of famine.

Read Psalm 33:18-19; Psalm 37:18-19; Job 5:19-27; Malachi 3:10-11.

>>> Some Christians make the mistake of giving people money or physical help but **without giving them the Good News of Christ**. People need to know how to be saved AND to walk in the prosperity and the health and the power of God. They need to know how to live a victorious life: how to have power over the world, the

flesh, and the devil! Other Christians make the mistake of giving people the Word of God, but **never helping them physically**. What does the Word of God tell you to do?

>>> Read James 2:15-17 again. It is talking about **a Christian brother or sister who is in need of the "necessities of life"—things needful to the body**. Not someone who is making a living by taking advantage of you ... or the saints. It is talking about a brother or sister in the Lord: someone who belongs to Christ, who needs help and who comes to you for help. Study carefully Deuteronomy 15:7-11. God, through Moses, gave instruction to Jews about taking care of their Jewish brethren who were poor and needy.

>>> **Satan would like to steal all your money by condemning you with guilt for not feeding the world (a hunger situation caused by the devil, himself, when he tempted man to separate himself from God in the Garden of Eden).** With all your money gone, you will then have nothing left with which to buy Bibles, or to help the saints in need, or to purchase media for the Gospel to be preached on TV, the Internet, or radio or in the newspapers. No money for CD's or DVD's to get out the gospel. No money left to buy bicycles to travel to villages with the Gospel. No money left to evangelize the lost or to teach the saints. No money left for you to get together with your Christian brothers and sisters and worship your Father God!

>>> So what do you do in a situation which involves another person's need? Here's your answer: If it is NOT a close Christian brother or sister as described in James 2:5-17, (God's Word already tells you what to do in that case), then your first action should be to PRAY:

1. Pray, and take the person to God, asking God to give them a miracle and to meet their need.

2. Pray, and ask God to show you what YOU should do, if anything, to help the other person (or people). God's answer to you will usually come in one of three ways, as outlined in A, B, or C below:

> A. "Do this..." (A certain specific action to take in order to help the other person in part or in full, either temporarily or permanently.)

> B. "Do whatever you feel you should; whatever is right according to the scriptures." (Read carefully Matthew 5:42 and Luke 6:30-36.)

> C. "Don't do anything!" (God may tell you to do something later on.)

**True spirituality is seeing a need
and meeting it.**

>>> Jesus said, *"Give to him who asks you, and do not turn from him who wants to borrow from you."* (Matthew 5:42) He also told us, *"Of him who takes away your goods, do not ask them back again ... but love your enemies, do good, and lend, hoping for nothing back again; and your reward shall be great, and you shall be the children of the Highest; for He is kind to the unthankful and to the evil. Therefore, you be merciful, like your Father also is merciful."* (Luke 6:30-36)

>>> You may feel that there is a conflict between #B and #C under Item #2 above. Not so! **The answer lies in priority and your responsibility under God**. A person may come to you to borrow $50 (or 50 Francs or 50 Cedi or 50 Pesos or 50 Lira or 50 Rupees) and you may have it in your possession; however, your priority may NOT be to loan either your friend or your enemy $50; it may be to take care of your responsibility—under God—to either your landlord or your family or your creditor, whichever the case may be.

>>> It is also possible that God may answer you with #A above and tell you to help a person, or to loan him $50, even though your family is hungry and you owe the landlord! **This is one of the times it is very important to know the voice of God: to know how to be led by the Spirit of God!** Time after time, God has asked me to give away all the money that I have had. However, on other occasions, God has told me, *"Don't do anything; this is a trick of the devil to steal your money!"* ... or ... *"Don't do anything; this is not a valid request!"*

165

One time a brother asked me for money for his family and I gave him everything I had ($1.42 USD). On the way home I thought, *"I should NOT have done that; I need that money to buy milk for my baby."* **Nobody knew that I gave him the money. (He lived in another county 30 miles away.) However, the next day I found 7 sacks of groceries at my front door.**

>>> Another example of priority and your responsibility under God—*as regards helping those in need*—might be as follows: Let's suppose someone comes to you and asks you for a certain amount of money; and let's suppose, also, that for several months you have been saving money so that you can buy a particular piece of equipment that you need for God's work: something that will help you reach more people for Christ. Or ...

Perhaps, you have been saving money for a particular evangelistic project—possibly to reach several million people with the message of Christ. **To whom is your priority in this case?** The millions of people who are lost and on their way to Hell? Or, the one person who needs physical help?

>>> Which is more important in regards to your responsibility to God: Obeying the Scriptural command of Jesus in Matthew 5:42, *"Give to him who asks you, and do not turn away from him who wants to borrow from you"* ... OR ... obeying the Scriptural Command of Jesus in the Great Commission, *"Go ... and teach (disciple) all nations."* If God has been leading you to save money to

reach people for Christ, would it not be unwise to then give it away? Rather, would it not be the devil wanting to take it away? **This is why you must know how to be led by the Spirit of God!**

Why are you in the ministry, or service, of God? First, you are to serve God; next, you are to serve mankind. *"The Son of Man (Yeshua) came not to be served, but to serve others."* You are to love God first; and then to love your neighbor as yourself. You can always PRAY for others and take them to God for a miracle. You can GIVE GOD'S WORD to others. Sometimes you can give PHYSICAL HELP to others.

The greatest work is to help people eternally; but it is also good if you can help them while they are here on earth. There are many ways to help a person here on earth, but the "highest way" is to help them to know God personally. Then ...

■ They can PRAY for themselves and for others.

■ Then, they can GIVE GOD'S WORD to others.

■ Then, they can give PHYSICAL HELP to others.

They will have God to help them, to lead them, to keep them alive in famine, and to help them to help others. God will be their Father!

True spirituality is "seeing a need and meeting it!"

FRUSTRATION AND YOUR FUTURE: THE WAY

When you are frustrated, many times you are sick; maybe not physically, but emotionally, spiritually, or financially.

There are seasons in your life—and there are certain **types** of seasons—such as economic downturns. This chapter is written to help you in these seasons.

We need to position ourselves daily—through faith—into the perfect center of God's will.

Have you ever thought: *"Why can't God keep me prosperous? Or, healthy? Or, victorious?"*

Or, maybe you questioned, *"WHY doesn't God send my MIRACLES to me now? WHY am I frustrated?"* This book will help you find the **perfect center** of God's will for your life.

There is a **spiritual** place of blessing for you, and a **geographic** place of blessing. **We need to be flexible in order to be powerful.**

At any given point on the axis of our relationship to God, **we need to ask of ourselves certain KEY questions**. The answer to these questions will help us to identify our position in the matrix of peace and productivity.

Also, **there are three KEY action-vertices that should align at any given time in your life**.

So—when frustration is invading you—back up one step and **analyze the situation.**

This section will help you to do that ... and to find the **healing** answer.

You're going to have a wonderful future!

"Are you WHERE God wants you to be?"

This chapter is written specifically to help you with frustration in the coming seasons of your life.

Someone reading this book right now is in a state of frustration. You are a servant of God—*and you are anointed of God*—but you are frustrated. The LORD has sent me to tell you: *"Hang in there. Your MIRACLES are on their way."*

I know what you're thinking: *"Well, WHY doesn't He send my MIRACLES now? WHY am I frustrated?"*

I will answer that: *"Because God is preparing your enemy."*

When the children of Israel left Egypt under the mighty deliverance of the Passover, they were then hemmed in between Migdol and the sea, with Pharaoh chasing them with 600 of his chosen chariots of war.

> *"And Pharaoh made ready his chariot, and took his people with him. And he took six hundred chosen chariots, and all the chariots of Egypt, and captains over every one of them. And the LORD hardened the heart of Pharaoh king of Egypt, and he pursued after the children of Israel."* (Torah: Exodus 14:6-8)

The children of Israel thought, *"Why can't God keep us delivered."* Someone reading this teaching has recently been thinking, *"Why can't God keep me prosperous? Or, healthy? Or, victorious?"*

He can, my friend. The same God that has delivered you in the past wants to deliver you again—and again—AND AGAIN.

The Israelites told Moshe:

> *"Because there were no graves in Egypt, have you taken us away to die in the wilderness? WHY have you dealt with us like this, to bring us out of Egypt?*
>
> *Is not this the word that we told you in Egypt, saying, 'Let us alone, that we may serve the Egyptians?' For it would have been better for us*

to serve the Egyptians, than that we should die in the wilderness." (Torah: Exodus 14:11-12)

I want to ask you a question: *"Are you WHERE God wants you to be?"*

We need to position ourselves daily—through faith—into the perfect center of God's will. We should do this in our prayer time, continuously throughout our life. It is not enough to tell our Heavenly Father that we want to be "IN" His will, but in faith we must decree to Him that we are positioning ourselves into the **perfect center** of His will. **We—*YOU and I*—have to do the positioning**.

When we pray *"Thy will be done,"* we are supplicating for the Father's will to be done *"in earth, as it is in Heaven."* We are asking for the provision of the spiritual logistics necessary for the Kingdom to be established on earth and for the millennial reign of Messiah to be implemented. However, **those who are involved in the front lines of spiritual warfare (leaders, rabbis, ministers, intercessors) must pray in a personal, yet practical, manner.**

We are in this conflict to WIN, and we must not lose sight of the fact that the souls of men and the destiny of nations **depend upon our victory**: individually, as part of an elite strike force unit.

At any given point on the axis of our relationship to God, we need to ask these basic questions:

171

- What should I do?

- How should I do it?

- Where (if any place) should I do it?

- When should I do it—or when should I go?

We need to be flexible in order to be powerful.

There is a **spiritual** place of blessing for you, and a **geographic** place of blessing. That is:

- A ministry, or work; and

- A place **WHERE** God wants you to minister, or work.

If you are preaching on the streets in Lome, Togo, and God wants you preaching on the streets in Aflao, Ghana, people will still be saved and God will still bless His Holy Word; however, the blessing in your personal life—or your ministry—will not be as great because you are NOT **where** God wants you!

We need to **maintain spiritual balance** at all times. For example, if God wants us to maintain a stable geographic location [i.e., fixed in a location geographically] and we move around not being obedient to His will, then we are sacrificing not only our inner peace, but also productivity in the Spirit.

On the other hand, if we become "set in concrete" in our ways, not willing to move—or maybe afraid to move—then we fall into the "snare" of the enemy. **We must be willing to leave our "comfort zone" at any time**. This assumes that we have spent adequate time in prayer: honestly seeking the Lord's will in the matter.

There is productive strength—as well as great inner peace—associated with being in the center of God's will. If you're not there, start today—**right NOW**—and experience REAL MIRACLES!

Pray with me NOW.

> *"Father in Heaven, I position myself by faith into the perfect center of your will, and I thank you for leading me. In the name of Messiah Jesus I pray. Amen."*

What you have to realize is that your enemy is not a leader of a **world** empire like Pharaoh. **Your enemy is stronger than Pharaoh**. Your enemy is a leader of a **universal** empire known as the Kingdom of Satan. This is WHY you must position your self into:

- The intersection of holy rest.

- The intersection of MIRACLES.

- The intersection of God's perfect will.

All three of these action-vertices should be concomitant—concurrent—in your life at any time. When you are in the center of God's perfect will for your life, you will experience God's rest and God's MIRACLES.

Your arch-enemy, the devil, does NOT want you to be in the perfect center of God's will for your life. And, he may use people—*even real Christians*—to work through at times, so that—*because of relational proximity*—you are perceiving your enemy as a person or people.

So when frustration is invading you, back up one step—**analyze the situation.** Analyze WHO and WHAT is blocking you—keeping you at a "dead end." Get up and do something about it. **It may be yourself that is blocking you.** Some people are their own greatest enemies. The problem is always "someone else." They have a "dead-end" mindset. My friend, if you are driving your automobile and find yourself at a dead end, that doesn't mean YOU are at a dead end! **GET OUT AND WALK.**

When you are frustrated, many times you are sick; maybe not physically, but emotionally, spiritually, or financially. And **the real reason you are sick and frustrated is because you are NOT trusting God.** You may even feel sick in your human spirit—your heart—and you feel "lean" in your soul because you're leaning on, or trusting, someone else **other than God.**

If you are leaning on someone other than God to take care of you and provide for you, then do NOT expect God to lead you!!!

God can take care of you any **way** and any **where**! I flew into Accra, Ghana, one time and a lady met me with a sack full of money. She said, *"Do you need any money."* If you have ever been to Ghana, West Africa, I think you will find this quite unusual ... possibly in the realm of MIRACLES.

When Rabbi Shaul (later the Apostle Paul, previously Saul of Tarsus) was on his way to Damascus to incarcerate and murder Christians, he was knocked down by a brilliant light from heaven.

*"And he fell to the earth, and heard a voice saying unto him, 'Shaul, Shaul, why do you persecute me?' And Shaul said, 'Who are you, Lord?' And the Lord said, 'I am Yeshua whom you persecute' ... And he trembled and was astonished and said, 'Lord, what do you want me to do?' And the Lord said unto him, '**Get up**, and **go into the city, and it will be told you what you must do.**'"* (Brit Chadashah: Acts 9:3-6)

That's what you have to do, my friend:

■ Pray;

■ Listen; and then,

■ **G—O—D.**

175

Go ...
Obey ... and,
Do!

Get up, my friend. **Go—Obey—Do**! Do NOT be concerned about your enemy. The LORD, Yeshua, has been preparing your enemy—*as he did Pharaoh*—to be wiped out. You see ... what you did NOT realize all this time was that **God has been preparing your enemy to launch you into your next phase of dominion—your next assignment of success—and has given you complete victory over your enemy**.

If you do not know Yeshua, you can NOW. Pray, and ask the God of Abraham, Isaac, and Jacob to reveal to you if Yeshua is really your Mashiach. When He does, then receive Him—obey Him—and live for Him. Pray this:

> *"God of Abraham, Isaac and Jacob, if Yeshua (Jesus) is really Your Son—the Messiah—please reveal Him to me and I will serve you the rest of my life. Please forgive my sins and take me to Heaven when I die."*

I'm going to share with you, also, another resource to help you not only to get out of your frustration, but help you create your future. It is my book, *Faith and Quantum Physics - Create Your Future*.

You're going to have a wonderful future, my friend!

UNLIMITED VISION WITH ATTAINMENT

In this chapter you will find the SECRETS of doing GREAT WORKS—unlimited works—for God. Do what you learn and you will NOT fail. Then, give God the glory: On earth ... and later in Heaven!

NOTICE: These principles transfer to any endeavor: business, social, family, military, and political.

The main thing people omit when establishing goals is NOT allowing for self-perpetuating growth or augmentation.

Never get so busy that you don't have time to dream! What is that **BIG** work you want to do for God? You CAN DO it!

Are you BELIEVING for the accomplishment of your vision through the years when you don't SEE fruit, production, or growth?

This section will provide you with KEYS and GUIDELINES to assure the attainment of your goals. Just DO what you learn.

Allow for self-perpetuating growth.

The title of this book may seem oxymoronic. **How can you have unlimited goals (vision) and succeed in accomplishing them?** Here is your answer:

By NOT limiting your goals. Usually **the main thing people omit when establishing goals is NOT allowing for self-perpetuating growth or augmentation.**

Years ago I gave three automobiles away to three different ministers of the Gospel. I had walked for three years before the Lord blessed me with the first auto I gave away; and I walked in between the time I gave the others away. I am now driving the ??th automobile (I forgot how many) that the Lord has given me. Seven of the autos were Cadillacs (the most expensive auto made in the USA) and in about half of them I had loudspeaker installations.

The Cadillacs were excellent for this setup because they had ample space between the front grille and the radiator to enable the sideways installation of a large 110 watt police horn speaker. Inside the cars were also installed amplifiers and secret (hidden) microphones. This way I could preach while driving and have both hands on my steering wheel. The sound was so loud from the loudspeaker that one time while driving down an interstate freeway, going about 70 mph, **the cattle in a field** a long way from the road even **turned to look as I was preaching**.

In large metropolitan cities I would preach while stopping at the red lights while the crowds of pedestrians would cross the street. **Sometimes people would risk getting run over and hurriedly walk (almost run) through (against) the red light just to get away from God's Word.**

One time while driving through the mountains the Lord impressed me to stop the car and preach on the loudspeaker. **There weren't any people or buildings around that I could see** but I obeyed anyway. I didn't know until a few minutes later that **there were men working down the mountainside building a house**. I preached to them from Hebrews 3:4, *"For every house is built by someone, but He who built all things is God."*

Whenever I'm home, in the morning I step out on the roof veranda and look at some of the most beautiful buildings in the world with architecturally superb designs. Amazed at their grandeur, I also reflect on all the planning, money, risk, coordination, and time that went into building them. And I always think of the verse in Hebrews 3:4, *"For every house is built by someone, but He who built all things is God."*

When I first look at the buildings, even with my engineering background, I think, *"How can men build these fantastic buildings?"* And then I think, *"But God built ALL things ... he made the men and the materials; and gave men the knowledge and skills needed to construct and finish them."*

179

I want to encourage you. **You can do something far BIGGER** than build buildings like these. **You can make disciples for Messiah Yeshua and MULTIPLY your ministry / vision through many future generations.**

First of all, never get so busy that you don't have time to dream! What is that **BIG** work you want to do for God? You CAN DO it!

"With men this is impossible, but with God all things are possible." [Matthew 19:26]

"If you can believe, all things are possible to him that believes." [Mark 9:23]

"And all things, whatever you shall ask in prayer, believing, you shall receive." [Matthew 21:22]

"For every house is built by someone, but He who built all things is God." [Hebrews 3:4]

Here is one of YOUR KEYS to success:

If your plans fit into God's plan ... you will have God's faith ... and God's faith always works!

This is one reason it is imperative to see the importance of Israel, Jerusalem, and God's chosen people—the Jews—in the divine plan of God.

"When the most High divided to the nations their inheritance, when He separated the sons of

Adam, He set the bounds of the people according to the number of the children of Israel. For the Lord's portion is His people; Jacob is the lot of His inheritance." [Deuteronomy 32:8-9]

Multiplication of ministry starts with the BELIEF in **the potential of one person**. This is where discipleship is important. K. Bruce Miller drives home this idea: *"Would you spend as much time preparing yourself to meet the needs of one person as you would preparing a sermon for five thousand? How much do you believe in the potential of one?"*

A few years ago I prophesied to my oldest daughter that she would start teaching God's Word. I bought her a new study Bible and gave it to her. About a month later she called me and told me that the Lord was having her start teaching. She and her husband and another couple started a home Bible study **with about 6 to 10 people**, alternating from each home. The other couple finally felt the Lord leading to start a church, and in about three years grew to 1,500 people attending. Around 400 of those attending were new Christians, having given their lives to the Lord within the previous year.

When you have a dream or vision that you want to accomplish for God, **the main thing you need to decide on at the outset is that you will NOT quit ... you will NOT give up!**

If you don't quit, you'll WIN!
But if you quit, you can't win!

Thomas Edison failed over 30,000 times before inventing the light bulb. The Bible says, *"A just man falls seven times, and rises up again."* [Proverbs 24:16]

You have **time**, **talent**, and **treasure** with which to serve the Lord. God is watching for your faithfulness. **Are you consistent in good times as well as bad?** Are you BELIEVING for the accomplishment of your vision through the years when you don't SEE fruit, production, or growth? **Does your plan fit into God's plan?**

Read Luke 11:5-15. Importunity means to keep on asking; approach God with your requests and be persistent and pressing.

> *"And I say unto you, Ask, and it shall be given to you; seek, and you shall find; knock, and it shall be opened unto you. For everyone that asks, receives; and he that seeks, finds; and to him that knocks, it shall be opened."* [Luke 11:9-10]

Have only super BIG, positive, more-than-maximum, unlimited goals. And—**keep enlarging them**. Refuse to have small, negative, limiting thoughts, dreams, and

182

visions. Say to yourself, *"I refuse to think or envision anything negative, small, minimal, or limited."*

Zechariah 4:10 says, *"For who has despised the day of small things?"* Don't worry about STARTING small ... just make sure the goal (the vision) is BIG and unlimited.

Associate with positive winners! **It would be better to be alone, and hang out with Jesus, than to associate with the wrong people.** There's an old saying, *"If you want to see what you'll become, look at the people with whom you associate."* This is **"the law of the group."** We associate ourselves with people we are like.

Find somebody who is positive and successful and spend quality time with them. If you can't find anyone like that, then spend lots of time with Jesus the Messiah—in fellowship, in His Word, and in prayer. **I always enjoy when I can be away from people so I can spend more time talking to Jesus.**

Project yourself into your visions and goals. **A successful hedging investor in the commodities futures market has to do two (2) things:**

- He has to mentally place himself in the trade; and,

- He has to ask himself, "Do I have the product or not?"

These two factors will determine the position a successful hedge investor will take. **It's the same way when you plan BIG works for God:**

- **You have to mentally place yourself in the vision.** See yourself at each stage of the growth. Then PLAN and PRAY accordingly. Pray ahead of time for each stage of development.

- **Ask yourself (ahead of time) at each stage of the project / vision: "Do I have what I need?"** If "Yes," pray and plan for the proper implementation. If "No," pray and receive in faith the people and things you need.

As your vision develops and comes to pass you will need a network. A **network** is comprised of:

- Logistics;

- Communication; and,

- Funding.

You need to pray ahead of time for these and receive them by faith. And **don't always look at the easy way**—or the path of least resistance. Also, **not every package that comes your way**—*that has your name on it*—**is necessarily from God**. It might be from the devil. It might be from a Christian. For example, you might receive an offer of funding or help from a Christian source, but make sure you pray about it before receiving

184

it. It may NOT be God's will. **I've given lots of money back to people after they gave it to me, and sometimes when it was offered to me.**

Read 2 Chronicles 25:9. King Amaziah had hired 100,000 mighty men to help him fight and had paid 100 talents of silver. Afterwards, the man of God told King Amaziah not to go carry out his plans to use these men. Amaziah then told the man of God, *"What shall we do for the 100 talents that I have given them?"* And the man of God answered him, *"But God is able to give you much more than this."*

■ How LARGE can you ASK?

■ How BIG can you THINK?

"Now unto Him that is able to do exceedingly abundantly above all that we ASK or THINK, according to the power that works in us ..." [Ephesians 3:20]

TRY THIS VISION

■ A Holy Spirit baptized church or Messianic synagogue in every neighborhood and village of the earth.

■ A Holy Spirit baptized witness in every house, home or family of the earth.

185

Take this message, my friend, and reach the whole world with the Good News of Jesus, the Messiah of Israel.

GIVING LIFE IS A PROCESS

You may be discouraged and ready to quit. Do NOT do it. There is a MIRACLE in this chapter for you. Your deliverance—your help—is on its way!

Adam and Eve were to replenish not only the Garden, but humankind. Not, necessarily "kind humans" but children! There's an old saying, *"It takes two parents to make one good child."*

This chapter is NOT about marriage nor is it about raising children. It is about producing offspring: both biological and spiritual. **It is about giving LIFE to others—even when it hurts.**

If you are a parent, you have undoubtedly experienced pain or sadness resulting from something that has happened to a child—or, maybe because of something a child did.

Giving life hurts, including giving spiritual life. Helping others know—and grow—in the LORD—but JOY overrides any pain attributed to the life process—if you know HOW to use the authority you have been given from the administrative Court of Heaven.

Giving life to others—*your biological children as well as your spiritual children*—sometimes hurts. But this section will tell you what to do so you can **experience POWER and finish with PRAISE** to God.

Giving life to others—*your biological children as well as your spiritual children*—sometimes hurts!

In the Bible we read, *"And the LORD God said, It is not good that the man should be alone; I will make him an help meet for him."* (Torah: Genesis 2:18)

Now the term "help meet" (or, "helper") means different things to different people:

- To Adam, it meant "Servant."

- To Eve, it meant "Men need help!"

- To God, it meant, "Vengeance is mine!" (That's a joke.)

But the original root meaning of that word in the original Hebrew language is "aw-zar," and it means "**to surround; to help**." (It's nice to have someone near to surround you at times, to help you.)

Notice the first command God gave to Adam and Eve: *"Be fruitful, and multiply, and replenish the earth, and subdue it."* (Torah: Genesis 1:28) They were to replenish

188

not only the Garden, but humankind. Not, necessarily "kind humans" but children!

There's an old saying, *"It takes two parents to make one good child."*

After I wrote my thesis, **I was told by two different doctors in two different states of the USA (in writing) the same as that I would never have children**. Like Abraham, I just believed God that He would give me a child. When the wife was not pregnant by two months after we were married I called an orphanage to see if we could adopt; but was turned down.

Well, finally about 18 months later I was working on the lawn and the wife came downstairs and told me, ***"I'm pregnant."*** I was so excited that I ran around a large city block praising God. It took me probably about five minutes. When I returned, the wife was crying because she thought that when she told me she was pregnant I ran away! Well, **I have had seven (7) children since the two written doctor's reports**. I should have sent them the bills!

Eve experienced the FIRST pains of childbirth. If you are a parent, you have undoubtedly experienced pains or sadness resulting from something that has happened to your child or children. **Giving life hurts, including spiritual life. However, helping others know—and grow—in the LORD produces JOY that overrides any pain attributed to the life process**.

One time, two of my daughters cut my hair—more correctly cut a hole in my hair—while I was sleeping. That was really a wonderful experience because I had to speak at a meeting in about two hours.

Another time, after an exhausting two weeks of outreach at the Olympics—while I was sleeping—two of my daughters put pink crème on my ears and were massaging them, trying to shape them like a Doberman's trimmed ears (pointed straight up!). I think they wanted me to tryout for StarTrek.

On another occasion, **one of my sons set the bed on fire underneath his mother while she was sleeping**. He is a pastor now. (I haven't figured that one out yet.) I wonder what—*not only sins, but stupid things*—we have done to our LORD, who is still pleased to call us His children.

The Bible tells us that Messiah Yeshua, because of the JOY set before Him, endured the pain of the cross-stake.

> *"Looking unto Jesus, the author and finisher of our faith; who for the JOY that was set before him endured the cross-stake, despising the shame, and is set down at the right hand of the throne of God."* (Hebrews 12:2)

Because the Messiah, Jesus, saw YOU and me having our sins forgiven because of what He was going to do—even with the suffering—on the cross-stake, He was willing to endure the PAIN and SUFFERING of the Roman crucifixion.

What is it that YOU are going through today, my friend? I'm aware that someone reading this section is about ready to quit. You have been mistreated, misunderstood and mismanaged ... but misinformed!

God has placed me in your path this day to tell you that it is NOT the people doing it to you ... it is Satan—your enemy—who is using the people. You are NOT reading this book by mistake!

The people who are attacking you are only instruments. **God will deal with them. Their feet shall slide in due time.**

But YOU must deal with the devil. And, I have GOOD NEWS for you! The LORD has given you authority over Satan. Use the name of Jesus and the Word of God against the devil. **The devil is NO match for you when you are under the anointing of God**. Jesus said, *"Behold, I give unto you power ... over all the power of the enemy: and nothing shall by any means hurt you."* (Luke 10:19)

He also said, *"Notwithstanding in this rejoice not, that the demons are subject unto you; but rather rejoice, because your names are written in Heaven."* (Verse 20)

Yeshua (Jesus) commanded YOU and me, His followers: *"Whatsoever you shall bind on earth shall **already have been bound** in heaven: and whatever you shall loose on earth shall **already have been loosed in heaven**."* (Literal Greek translation from the Brit Chadashah, Hebrew New Testament: Matthew 18:18)

Messiah Yeshua did an **unassisted triple play** on a man who was:

■ Demon possessed;

■ Blind; and,

■ Could not speak.

Immediately, the religious leaders accused Yeshua of casting out demons by the prince of demons (Satan). Jesus answered them, *"How can one enter into a strong man's house, and spoil his goods, except he first bind the strong man? And then he will spoil his house."* In other words:

■ Bind Satan first,

■ Then go after his demons.

Go after the demons who tell lies about you, or attack your finances, or your integrity—or who try to hinder you in anyway. **Bind the strong man (Satan) and cast him out along with his demons that try to hinder you**.

Here's WHAT to do:

- **First**, PRAY and plead (as in a LEGAL court pleading) the BLOOD of Messiah (or, Christ) over your situation.

- **Second**, COMMAND the devil and his demons in the name of JESUS to depart ... tell the devil and his evil spirits that Jesus is your LORD and you now APPLY the BLOOD of Jesus Christ against Satan and his hosts. **Say it like this**:

    "Satan ... Jesus, the Messiah of Israel, is my LORD, and I APPLY His BLOOD that was shed on the cross stake for my sins against you, Satan, and against all of your demons that would try to hinder me. I cast you and your demons out—away—from hindering me, and I remind you, Satan, of your future: which is Hell, the Lake of Fire ... forever."

Friend, if your life goals are set around ETERNAL things, things that last—*like helping others to find The Way to Heaven*—then you will at times experience some pain or hurt. But remember, *"Weeping may endure for the night, but JOY comes in the morning."* (Psalm 30:5)

Giving life to others—your biological children as well as your spiritual children—sometimes hurts. However, you always have power over the devil and his demons in the name of Jesus, the One Who gives you the authority.

193

But remember, your real JOY should come from the fact that your name is written in Heaven—PLUS—the names of those who receive the Lord through your help are also written down in Heaven.

"The JOY of the LORD is your strength."
– Nehemiah 8:10

DON'T LET THE LITTLE DOGS BOTHER YOU

There are several strategies, tricks, and diversionary tactics of the enemy **to halt, hinder, impede, nullify or destroy** your profession, your ministry or your reputation.

Situations that arise where people gossip or lie about you are usually from either of two sources: a vindictive spirit or a spirit of jealousy

---

One of the strategies or tricks of the enemy is to use people—or, get them—to attack you through lies, false accusations (or, true ones), or gossip.

A "gossip"—a person who gossips—is defined as "**a person who likes talking about other people's private lives in a chiefly derogatory manner.**"

It is interesting to note that the word "devil" is from the Greek "diabolos" and means "**a traducer: one who attacks the reputation of another by slander or libel**," and is synonymous with "backbiter, slanderer, defamer."

This chapter will explain HOW and WHY these attacks are generated against YOU—and what to do about them so you can be FREE and live in VICTORY.

PLUS ... included are references to resources **to help you increase your future production** so you can turn around any past attacks from the enemy and "make him pay."

If he hollers ...

make him pay ...

50 souls every day!

I delivered newspapers at the ages of 11 and 12. I would start collecting from the customers on Thursdays so I could pay my bill on Saturday morning and then buy a hamburger and go to the movies. Usually on the deliveries I would throw the folded newspapers onto the porches from the sidewalk. This was not always possible, so sometimes (especially when I wanted to collect money) I would have to go into the yard. **Lots of times these yards were fenced because of mean dogs**.

God always protected me. Near the end of my morning route, about sunrise, I had to go to a home where there was a very mean red English Chow. On the corner just before I would arrive at this house, a white Boxer (dog) would meet me and finish the route with me. The boxer kept the Chow from bothering me and hurting me.

The dogs that were the most bothersome were the little dogs. They would snap at my feet and legs and many times grab hold of my trousers with their teeth.

However, **I learned just to shake them off.** I have found through the years that it is the same way in the Christian walk: shake the "little dogs" off. The "little dogs" represent the people who lie or gossip about you. **When people lie or gossip about you, just shake them off.**

For several years during the early 1970's I lived a few blocks from Richard and Karen Carpenter—*The Carpenters.* One of my favorite songs they recorded was: *We've Only Just Begun.* We had a mutual friend who owned a stationery store where Karen Carpenter and I used to do business. (By God's grace, I led the owner of that store to Christ at the counter one day and he became a wonderful Christian.)

Karen died at the age of 33 of heart failure caused by anorexia nervosa in the city of Downey (Los Angeles area) where I still have an office. She had struggled for eight years with chronic anorexia. Karen had been down to 79 pounds in weight, and started back up to 110, but died one year later.

What most people don't know is this: A radio personality one time referred to Karen as **"Richard's chubby little sister." Those words went out into eternity with Karen.**

Situations that arise where people gossip or lie about you are usually from either of two sources: a vindictive spirit or a spirit of jealousy. **It may even be a loved one who performs such actions.** What you have to realize is that the "instrument"—whatever or whomever is the channel through whom the attack flows—is just that: an "instrument."

There are several strategies, tricks, and diversionary tactics of the enemy to halt, hinder, impede, nullify or destroy your profession or ministry or your reputation.

You must always be cognizant of this fact. There is a devil who has planned stratagem, and who has forces (spirits) of intelligence monitoring your plans, your progress, and your private relationships.

One of the strategies or tricks of the enemy is to use people—or, get them—to attack you through lies, false accusations (or, true ones), or gossip.

A "gossip"—a person who gossips—is defined as "a person who likes **talking about other people's private lives in a chiefly derogatory manner**." The Holy Bible also talks about "busybodies," which in the original Greek means **"to meddle, to work all around"** and sometimes refers to the **"curious arts" or the "works of Satan."** The devil is actually the source of gossip,

198

whether true or false, and merely uses—or **works through—the "instrument."**

It is interesting to note that the word "devil" is from the Greek "diabolos" and means "a traducer: one who attacks the reputation of another by slander or libel," and is synonymous with "**backbiter, slanderer, defamer.**"

Especially egregious is the action of a Christian, one who claims to know Christ, who talks about another person in a defaming way, working around as a busybody—a gossip—about other people's private lives. So repugnant is this action to the Lord that **the Holy Spirit equates it to being a "murderer or a thief or an evildoer."** *"But let none of you suffer as a murderer, or a thief, or as an evildoer, or as a busybody in other men's matters."* (Brit Chadashah: 1 Peter 4:15)

A "busybody" includes someone who brings up material from many years past that is either non-relevant to today because of the BLOOD of Christ purging it—or is either false or an exaggeration. A "jealous" person is a person who is "envious of someone else's achievements or advantages." People are never jealous of you unless you are either doing more than they are or have more than they have (which can include "gifts" or "operations" of God Spirit).

Here is a quote that sums up the picture very nicely: *"Criticism, condemnation, and complaint are creatures of the wind. They come and go on the*

breath of lesser beings and have no power over me."
(Author unknown.)

My friend, remember to shake off the "little dogs."

If people are jealous of YOU—especially God's People—it is usually because you have a strong gifting from God and the enemy of your soul is "stirring" them up against you to either discourage YOU ... or to get you to quit. Remember, it is the devil who is the source of the opposition and resistance, not the instrument—the people—he is using. **Pray for the people.**

Remember when Jesus was asleep in the boat during a violent storm?

Notice what happened and what He did.

> And the same day, when it was evening time, Jesus said unto them, *"Let us pass over unto the other side."*
>
> And when they had sent away the multitude, they took him even as he was in the ship. And there were also with Him other little ships.
>
> And there arose a great storm of **wind**, and the **waves** beat into the ship, so that it was now full.
>
> And he was in the back part of the ship, asleep on a pillow: and they awakened him, and said unto him, *"Master, don't you care that we perish?"*

And he arose, and **rebuked the wind,** and **said unto the sea,** *"Peace, be still."* And the wind ceased, and there was a great calm.

And he said unto them, *"Why are you so fearful? How is it that you have no faith?"*

And they feared exceedingly, and said one to another, *"What manner of man is this, that even the **wind** and the **sea** obey him?"*

– Mark 4:35-41

NOTICE: After the disciples awakened him, Jesus did TWO (2) things:

- He rebuked the wind;

- He said unto the sea.

The gale force of the wind caused the violent waves to beat against the boat. That is, **the waves were a result of the tempestuous wind**. Either—the wind OR the waves—could have resulted in extreme peril: even death to the disciples.

This is an extremely important principle you need to exercise every day of your life. **In the Name of Jesus** the Messiah (the Christ), you need to:

- **Command every WORK—*every opposition and resistance*—against you** (including your family, your business, your ministry) **to cease and desist**.

Then ... because **there may be PROCESSES that have started because of the initiating WORK**—opposition and resistance—you need to:

■ **Command every PROCESS that has started** as a result of the initiating work **to cease and desist forever!**

So now—in addition to praying for the people—you know what else to do.

Below are three (3) resources (books) to help you in your work for God. (See Book List at end of book.)

■ *Action Keys for Success*

■ *How to do Great Works*

■ *Success Cycles and Secrets*

You can NOT miss with the above books! This is a **great** way to confuse your enemies and **bless** those around you ... including the many people—*nations also included*—that God will reach through you. Let that **IDEA** God has given you come to pass.

Then let God anoint YOUR IDEA for **great works**—and don't stop with one success—go for **repeat success**.

You can do it in the name of the LORD while shaking off the little dogs.

There are four major sectors of Boolean commonality that have marked overlays **dealing with the entry into the Last Days: forerunners of the End Times**. Three (3) of these sectors have a highly positive correlation with relation to the former President of the United States, Barack Obama.

For those of you who are not acquainted with the University of Excellence—*UofE*—here is the mission statement:

The University of Excellence is an online study forum for the end times enabling the serious seeker with advanced instruction, intel, and prophecy for personal growth, cross cultural communications, and international strategies.

All sectors of the geopolitical spectrum are analyzed for Boolean logic commonalities in relation to trends and issues. Those with highly positive correlation of linear regression are brought into focus and subject to more critical analysis.

The four specific sectors—*The Four F's of the End Times*—covered by this chapter, are as follows:

- Family Fidelity

- Fallen Spirits

- False Treaties

- False Messiah

It is the purpose of this teaching to provide you with a skeletal acquaintance of these sectors so that you may know:

- Where you're at;

- Where you're going;

- Know what's happening today; and,

- Know what's happening in the future.

Be like the Berean believers and the sons of Issachar: search the scriptures AND have an understanding of the times!

FAMILY FIDELITY

Lots has been written of the unfaithfulness of men as the head of the family unit; however, not much concerning infidelity as associated with the woman (the wife or mother). There can be several reasons for infidelity on the part of the wife:

- Way of revenge;

- Boredom and curiosity; and,

- Proving they are still desirable

- Cheating for change or breakup

- Chasing a dream of ideal romance

However, the man (the husband or father), as a model of God, is to be not only a strong leader ... but also a healer thru:

- Intimacy

- Discipline

- Love

- Value

It takes a STRONG person to override the infidelity of the other mate; however, this can be carried out even by a "weak" person who trusts in the "strength" of God. *"Let the weak say 'I am strong.'"* (Tanakh: Joel 3:10)

CAVEAT: Many times the offended mate "rebounds" and commits the same infidelity as "payback." The key determinants should be:

What is BEST for —

- The Kingdom of God;

- The family; and,

- The future.

However, under the emotions of hurt, anger, jealousy and the desire for revenge, the wisdom to do the right thing is not often heeded.

I knew a minister with a strong anointing of God who was deceived by evil spirits and committed adultery several times with different women. When he realized by the direction of the Holy Spirit that it was for the good of the children to have TWO parents, he tried to make amends and bring the family back together with healing ... but by that time **the wife had a boyfriend sleeping with her in the house with the children and a couple of "druggies" living in the garage**. The mother, who claimed to be a Christian, refused to forgive and allow the family to be back together, and subsequently filed for divorce. This absolutely threw the children into turmoil.

There are two key principles here:

- It's hard to submit to a person you don't RESPECT; and,

- You can't sacrifice what you have LOST.

Had the wife in the true-life example above simply obeyed the scriptural admonition for Christians—God's believers—in 1 Corinthians 7:10-11 the family unit would have been saved and the children would have SEEN living proof of God's restoration power and love.

"Now to the married I command, yet not I but the Lord: a wife is not to depart from her husband.

But even if she does depart, let her remain unmarried or be reconciled to her husband. And a husband is not to divorce his wife."

I don't need to share the statistics with you that today HALF of Christian marriages end in divorce. But let me share something with you that should wake you up!

POSTULATE #1: Two (2) of the four (4) sectors of Boolean commonality we are discussing in this teaching are—or will be—directly related in the Last Days (the End Times of Planet Earth) to the first sector discussed here, Family Fidelity. Those two are as follows:

- Fallen Spirits, and

- False Messiah.

POSTULATE #2: The previous President of the USA, Barack Obama, had an "overlay" of a highly positive correlation of linear regression to the following:

- Disruption of Family Fidelity; and,

- Patterns of social underpinning attributed to the coming False Messiah (the anti-Christ).

EDITOR'S NOTE – Before you judge this strictly objective study or any personal association to me as the writer-reporter, please note TWO things: **1.** I am NOT a

Republican, Democrat or Libertarian. I have voted for all three of these parties in the past; and **2**. I prayed for President Obama, his wife Michelle, and their daughters Malia and Sasha every day while he was in office. How about you?

There were patterned socialization characteristics of the above-mentioned two postulates. But for now, let's continue with both analyses and prophecies concerning the "The Four F's of the End Times."

FAMILY FIDELITY: We have discussed the family fidelity sector in a practical yet spiritual aspect above. But now let me speak prophetically. A great dichotomy of offensives will soon start to happen in the FAMILY structure. At the same time the true family structure of man and woman is being eroded by same sex marriage, there will be a revitalization of holy family structures: a revival—a spiritual bonding—a godly melting together of the REAL family. **Many previously divorced couples will re-unite in marriage**. Many family and inter-personal relationships will be healed.

There will be the ministry of Elijah the prophet that will *"turn the hearts of the fathers to the children and the hearts of the children to their fathers."* (Tanakh: Malachi 4:5-6)

FALLEN SPIRITS: There will be satanic combinations: "demonic doubles" working increasingly in the end-times.

Demonic Double #1 – Islam and politically oriented leftist-socialists. These will work unwittingly with Islam for a while ... until which time the Islamic Caliphate starts attacking them, also. Why do leftists work with Islamists? Because they both hate Jews and real Christians, the nation of Israel and the USA foundations based upon Judeo-Christian heritage.

Demonic Double #2 – Religion and Demons. These will establish strongholds in the European Union and work from within to then attack outwardly against Israel, the Jews and real Christians.

Here's a "sleeper" for you to watch: Germany. Just as under Nazi control during World War II, many people did NOT speak up against the political attacks against real Christians and Jews—especially the Jews—**this type of attack will increase in Germany**. You will see that Hungary, Portugal and Poland are also becoming more anti-Semitic. WHY? The same regional strongholds of religion and demons—*working in combination*—become synergistic in their offensives.

The same demon spirits that operated in Nazi Germany are still ALIVE today. Demons do NOT die. **They are disembodied spirits that seek to inhabit live bodies: human or animal.**

MY PROPHECY: **A dichotomy of spiritual offensives will evolve from Germany.** One will be powerful and apostolic prophetic ministries who will preach to millions. The other will be end-time works orchestrated for use by anti-Christ to suppress Jews and real Christians in the end-time.

Fallen spirits will begin to inter-breed with humans—*while at the same time*—through use of genome altering implants on "willing" subjects to prepare a "submissive leadership core" for the anti-Christ as he implements his system of political, economic and military control on Planet Earth. **These "willing subjects" MAY be from a DOUBLE source:**

- **Source #1** – Politically expedient recipients of the *"Mark of the Beast: his mark, or his name, or the number of his name."* Those who will take the "mark" so they can buy or sell or carry on commerce; and, those who did not want to be beheaded for not taking the mark. (See Brit Chadashah: Revelation Chapter 13.)

- **Source #2** – Some believe another source will be from willing subjects of alien abduction who receive genome altering implants. However, <u>I do NOT believe this</u> (but, it is a possibility). There are other more scripturally based options as to HOW people may receive the genome altering implants or hybridization.

Much research is being carried out today in areas of development of a "hybrid" species: i.e., harvesting of human fetuses. Study the book, *Enhanced Humans: Mystery Matrix* by Prince Handley for complete overview of this subject.

Remember, there was gene pool corruption in Noah's day. The "sons of God" took wives of those whom they chose. (Notice: the "sons of God" never refers to "believers" in the Tanakh, the Old Testament.) This resulted in God destroying the whole earth by the Great Flood; only 8 righteous souls were left: Noah, his wife, his three sons and their wives.

1 Peter 3:19-20, 2 Peter 2:4-5 and Jude 6 refer to the fallen angels who procreated with the daughters of man in the Days of Noah (before the Flood). This resulted in the "Nephilim:" "the fallen ones"—or—"ones who cause others to fall." We know from scripture that the "fallen angels" who took to themselves the "daughters of men"—associated time wise with the Days of Noah and the Great Flood—have been bound in everlasting chains for their just judgment of everlasting fire.

However, the offspring of the "fallen angels" —the Nephilim—were drowned in the Great Flood. That is, **their bodies drowned; however, their spirits could be the demons we read about in the Brit Chadashah (the New Testament). Demons never die!**

The development of a hybrid species in the end times—through which the anti-Christ MAY derive his submissive leadership core—could well be the result of fallen spirit forces (demons) facilitating the same, rather than aliens from another planet. **These fallen spirit forces (demons) may be from extra-dimensional time-space—not from other planets—but from a megaverse** (outside our traditional concept of space-time continuum).

FALSE TREATIES: These are treaties designed by Satan to prepare the way for the reception of his agent: the false messiah (anti-Christ). These are treaties based upon "wind." They have NO substance—they are or may be easily broken—and have no practical or pragmatic "teeth."

One typical example is the recent agreement between USA, Russia and Syria (Obama and Putin) concerning the destruction of chemical weapons. Another will probably be the Joint Comprehensive Plan of Action (JCPOA) signed in Vienna July 14, 2015, between Iran and the P5+1 (the five permanent members of the United Nations Security Council—China, France, Russia, United Kingdom, United States—plus Germany), and the European Union).

Just as a side note, I told Israel in August, 2008, NOT be deceived by (then) current peace talks by Olmert and Assad. At that time Obama and US wanted to force Israel into negotiations with Damascus. I warned Israel

NOT to do it. Listen to (or read show notes) of my podcast: *"Israel, New Forces in Middle East Parlance."*

False treaties will increasingly be made between sharply contradicting nations, cultures, philosophies and national interest groups. The stated mission of the **U of E**—*University of Excellence*—is to utilize Boolean logic to analyze such happenings in current geopolitical processes. The mainstream populace of the world is uneducated regarding geopolitical processes.

FALSE MESSIAH: I believe the "false messiah" (anti-Christ) is alive today. I also believe he is operating in governmental and geopolitical circles today. I believe he does NOT yet know exactly his role as governed by Satan. I believe he has NOT yet been incarnated by Satan. However, I believe he willingly deceives the populace over whom he governs, as well as other nations and has—even at this time—the goal of "world leader." This goal will finally morph into the goal of "world domination" as his body becomes overtaken and incarnated by Satan.

The "false messiah" will claim to solve the world's problems, to heal the Israeli-Arab land dispute and allow the Jews to build their temple in Jerusalem on the Temple Mount.

When the coming world leader—*appointed by the New Global Government*—takes over, he will make a treaty (a covenant) with Israel for seven years. Today, in addition to disease and famine issues, the leaders of the dominant nations are concerned with three (3) primary factors:

- Attaining peace among nations and ethnic groups;

- Guaranteeing the flow of oil; and,
  Stopping terrorism and conflict in the Middle East (especially between Israel and the Palestinians).

- And the chief bargaining factor will be the city of Jerusalem.

Remember, the false messiah (the anti-Christ) will make a seven year treaty with Israel, and in the middle of the seven years he will break the treaty, go into the Jewish Temple—which he will allow to be built on the Temple Mount in Jerusalem as part of the stipulations of the treaty—and **42 months later desecrate it by declaring that he is god**. This will begin the worst "Holocaust" the Jewish People and Israel have ever experienced.

SUMMARY: The four F's to watch for are —

- Family Fidelity;

- Fallen Spirts;

- False Treaties; and,

■ False Messiah.

Now you know HOW to discern the times with accuracy. Teach your friends!

Watch and pray ... that you may be accounted worthy to stand before the Son of Man (Jesus the Messiah) and to escape the things that are coming upon the earth. Above all, if you do NOT know the Messiah, PRAY and ask Him into your life as your LORD; ask Him to direct you and fill you with His Holy Spirit (Ruach HaChodesh).

Pray this prayer:

> *"God of Abraham, Isaac and Jacob ... if Yeshua (Jesus) is really my Messiah, please reveal Him to me, and I will serve Him the rest of my life. Help me to live for you here on earth and take me to Heaven when I die. Amen."*

YOUR GREATEST REWARD OPPORTUNITY

Some of the most powerful things in God's Kingdom are the simplest.

In this chapter you will learn how to reach nations for the LORD and how to bring the healing, apostolic power of God to individuals.

You will learn how to impact the earth and—*as a result*—reap great and huge rewards in Heaven PLUS ... you will prosper, have great favor, and be materially enriched in the earth.

Hang on! You're about to experience power, peace and prosperity!

*"Whatever you bind on earth **shall already have been bound in Heaven**; and whatever you loose on earth **shall already have been loosed in Heaven**."*

How would you like to have some of the GREATEST rewards handed out in Heaven?

Rewards that you can give back to the Master at His feet!

217

Some of the most powerful things in God's Kingdom are the simplest.

Let me share with you something you can do that will be SUPER EFFECTIVE in:

- Evangelism;

- Raising up new Churches and/or Messianic Synagogues;

- Reaching the nations for Messiah; and;

- Bringing the healing and apostolic power of Messiah to individuals.

In Matthew 12, verses 12-29, Jesus said, *"I cast out devils by the Spirit of God. How can one enter into a strong man's house (or, the devil's house), and spoil his goods, except he first BIND the strong man? And then he will spoil his (the devil's) house."* The binding and loosing power of the Church is one of the teachings of Messiah Jesus. Jesus said, *"Whatever you shall bind on earth shall be bound in Heaven; and whatever you shall loose on earth shall be loosed in Heaven."* (Matthew 18:18)

In the original language of the text, **the actual meaning of this text is as follows**: *"Whatever you bind on earth **shall already have been bound in Heaven**; and whatever you loose on earth **shall already have been loosed in Heaven**."*

In graduate studies in different theological seminaries I attended we were NOT taught such things, even though they were some of the best conservative seminaries. However, one day a Chinese professor—who was also a good Hebrew scholar and president of another seminary—told us about HOW he had bound Satan and **cast out demons from a dwelling in China where Buddha had been worshipped**. That opened my eyes!

Years ago the Lord began to minister to me about the binding and loosing power of the church. A short while afterward, I flew to the eastern part of the USA to hold a seminar at a Baptist church. The pastor picked me up at the airport and during the trip to his home we put the car onto a ferry and crossed a river.

During that time he told me an amazing thing. He said, *"Recently, the lord has been dealing with me about the binding and loosing power of the church."* (He didn't know the Lord had been showing me the same thing.) He began to tell me about the many miracles they had seen as a result.

About six months after that, I had just returned from Africa where I had been ministering for five weeks. As soon as I returned home I received a phone call from a pastor who asked me to come meet a missionary family from the Indo China / Burma area. I was very weary and needed rest; however, I felt the Lord wanted me to meet them.

There were three in the family: grandfather, father, and grandson. Together, they had labored in that demonized area for over 50 years, and had been imprisoned by the Communists. They told me an even more amazing story. They had seen very little fruit (souls saved) during the whole **time of their ministry, starting with the grandfather.**

One day, the Lord instructed them to start "binding" Satan and casting him out of the areas where they had been—and were to be—ministering. They began to see many people being saved.

Next, the Lord instructed them to start "loosing" the Holy Spirit into these same areas. In not too long a time **they baptized more than 50,000 new converts**. You can read about their story in the book, *Exodus from a Hidden Valley*, published by Reader's Digest. However, the story had been "watered" down somewhat due to the readership niche.

PRAY IN THIS MANNER

Use the "Binding and Loosing" authority of the Church. **Bind Satan and his demons, and evil works and workers in the name of Jesus and cast them out of areas and domains**.

Ask God to pour out His Spirit on every nation, tribe, tongue, and dialect—on every strata of society: political; educational; religious; media; the arts; business and commercial; martial, military and police forces; civil authorities, leaders and servants.

Loose the Holy Spirit into every area and strata of society. Ask the Lord to raise up a great Holy Spirit baptized Church and / or a great Messianic Synagogue in every neighborhood and village of the earth ... and a great Holy Spirit baptized witness in every house or family of the earth.

AGREE WITH ME

Following the example(s) which Jesus taught us in Luke 11:5-8 and Luke 18:1-8, every day for years I have prayed for certain specific things. I won't share most of them as they are personal; however, the LORD commanded me to share part of my daily prayer(s) with you—and to INVITE YOU to agree with me daily in some of these specific areas.

The LORD also commanded me to:

> "*Tell my people that **if they do this faithfully they will impact the earth more greatly** than in any endeavor they have taken part of previously. Also**, they will reap great and huge rewards** in Heaven as a result of this agreement. In days and years to come, those who are faithful in this prayer agreement **will also prosper, have great favor, and be materially enriched in the earth.**"*

Below are five (5) items, part of what I pray for daily:

"Father in Heaven, in Jesus' name:

1. *I **bind** the devil and cast him out of every nation, tribe, tongue and dialect of Planet Earth;*

2. *I **cast** the devil out and away from the rulers and leaders of Planet Earth: every type of ruler and leader in every strata of society;*

3. *I **loose** the Holy Spirit into every nation, tribe, tongue and dialect of Planet Earth and upon all the rulers and leaders of earth: every type of ruler and leader in every strata of society;*

4. *I **loose** one or more great Holy Spirit baptized Churches and/or Messianic Synagogues into every neighborhood and village of the earth;*

5. *I **loose** one or more great Holy Spirit baptized witnesses into every house, home or family of the earth."*

If you want to pray even more specifically, go to "Key Nations" at www.realmiracles.org/global.html where we have listed the 100 Key Nations for which you can direct prayer. You can also obtain other resources and strategies in the following two books for advanced missions:

The Art of Christian Warfare

New Global Strategy

Agree with me in these same areas **FAITHFULLY** and watch what starts to happen! The MIRACLES of God are aimed at you from every direction!

It's fun to pray ... it works!

P.S. - Also, I regularly "loose" in the name of Messiah Jesus the following: *"Great Holy Spirit baptized apostles, prophets, evangelists, pastor-rabbis and teachers INTO all the great Holy Spirit baptized Churches and Messianic Synagogues being raised up."* (You may do this, also, if you like.)

Whether you're a business leader, a housewife, a student or an entrepreneur—if you're involved in God's PLAN and PURPOSE—God WANTS to do GREAT MIRACLES for you and through you!

One thing you may be overlooking—**and which can increase you productivity AND your joy**—is that you should be not only developing your life skills ... but sharing them.

When you discover the centrality of purpose AND the secret plan for your calling, you will begin to see the **barriers removed and miracles happen** to enable you to implement as many NEW works as you can conceptualize.

This chapter will help you to change your thinking. **It will help you to think BIG**. *"But new wine must be put into new bottles; and both are preserved."* (Luke 5:38)

This section will help you to think PAST the limits of your mind—to stretch out your horizon of ENDEAVORS and THOUGHTS—**to color outside the lines.**

"These things began Jesus both to DO and to TEACH."

You are a leader. If you were not ... you would not be reading this section. Since you are a leader, why not learn from a leader? His name is Joshua. You are to conquer like Joshua. You have the same God—and the same Holy Spirit —and the same Commander of the Armies of the LORD.

You are to divide the land—*the inheritance*—by teaching those you lead how you won—*and by teaching them the authority by which you won*—so they can conquer and win, too.

Joshua was Moses' Chief aide and military leader. He became Israel's leader after Moses' death. Joshua led the people across the Jordan River and into the Promise Land.

Seven (7) nations were destroyed in the land. After the conquest of the land by the children of Israel, the land was divided among the tribes of Israel.

There were tremendous MIRACLES in Joshua's day:

- The crossing of Jordan;

- The fall of Jericho; and,

- The sun standing still.

NOTE: All these miracles had to do with getting God's people into the land and driving out the enemy! They were involved in God's plan and purpose—which was ultimately to bring forth the Messiah through the seed line of the Jews.

If you're involved in God's PLAN and PURPOSE to reach the world for Messiah, God will do GREAT MIRACLES for and through you!

Remember: The KEY to the Old Testament: "A record of a nation designed to bring forth a Man (the Messiah of God)." The KEY of the New Testament is: "A record of a Man (the Messiah of God) designed to bring forth a nation (the people of God)."

For this purpose the Son of God was manifested, that He might destroy the works of the devil.

Your job is the same as Joshua's. To go into new territory and conquer for the LORD: to destroy the works of the devil; and then to divide the land (inheritance) among God's people.

Let me repeat: "How do YOU divide the land among God's people?" Here's your answer, **"By teaching them their authority in Christ—WHO they are in Christ and WHAT they have in Christ—by teaching them HOW you conquered, and sharing the blessings you have received, so they will know how to conquer: HOW TO WIN!**

Do you have your orders from God like Moses and Joshua? **Are you operating in the perfect center of God's will for your life?** If not, **pray and ask God to show you His plan for your life.** Spend time ALONE with God daily in your prayer closet (a regular place where you can meet with Him). If your plan fits into God's plan, you will have God's faith: and God's faith always works!

READ IT AGAIN:

If your plan fits into God's plan ...
you will have God's faith ...
and God's faith always works.

TO LEAD A GREAT BODY OF PEOPLE, SEEK GOD'S ADVICE & FOLLOW IT!

Moses led over 3,000,000 people through the wilderness. Multiply the male census (603,550) by 2 (allowing each man a wife) = 1,200,000 and then figure 3 children (minimum) for every family (3 X 600,000 = 1,800,000). Whenever a major problem arose, Moses prayed and talked to God about it **before he took action**.

The one time he acted foolishly, **when he did not take God's advice**, cost him earthly blessings. He became angry so that he "hit" the rock instead of "speaking" to it. Forty years earlier, God had told him to HIT the rock and water would come out for the people to drink.

227

However, near the end of the wilderness wanderings, when the people were complaining over thirst again, God told Moses only to SPEAK to the rock and water would come out. Moses became angry and, even though the fault was with the people he was leading, the Bible says:

"He spoke UNADVISEDLY with his lips." (He called them a bunch of rebels.) Read Exodus 17:1-7; Numbers 20:1-13; and Psalm 106:32-33.

- Make **your plan** fit into **God's plan**.

- Seek God's advice and follow it.

- Teach people their authority in Christ. (Divide the land among God's people.)

RECEIVING MIRACLES FOR THE IMPOSSIBLE WORK

*"He will glorify Me, for He will take of what is Mine and declare it to you. **All things that the Father has are Mine**. Therefore I said that He will take of mine and declare it to you."* (John 16:14-15)

Are you having trouble believing for GREAT THINGS—impossible things—in your life and ministry? How big can you **THINK**? How big can you **ASK**?

Make sure your plans and your goals go BEYOND what YOU can do. When you enter the realm of impossibility, then you are in God's realm: the realm of MIRACLES. Then, He will be the only one who can receive the glory!

Don't hesitate to BELIEVE BIG!

---

*"Now to Him who is able to do **exceedingly abundantly above** ALL that we ASK or THINK, according to the power that works in us."* (Ephesians 3:20)

You can START those new works for God—for His glory—throughout your life. Just follow the precepts you learn in this chapter and be willing to be hidden according to God's will. **Stay under the radar as much as possible.**

REMOVE THE BARRIERS

Remove the constrictions. Expand your circles of influence. Break the old barriers. Expand your touch. Use your faith. God will bring it to pass.

People need the breath of God—the touch of God. **You are the instrument of God to reach people**. Even your prayers for every nation, tribe, tongue, and dialect of the earth to be emblazoned with the glory of God are tools of LOVE and POWER through which the Holy Spirit works to reach people in time and space: sometimes years later in time—and continents away in space.

I have known God to use media broadcasts that were produced years before as instruments through which people were saved, healed, baptized in the Spirit, and received MIRACLES. **God honors His Word. He watches over it to perform it**. *"Then said the LORD unto me, You have well seen: for I will hasten my word to perform it."* (Jeremiah 1:12)

Your personal sphere of influence—through leadership, through ministry, through prayers, through giving—is at the threshold of increase in quantum leaps dependent upon what you do with what you learn in this section. So be it, according to **YOUR** faith.

"Enlarge the place of your tent. And let them stretch out the curtains of your dwellings; do not spare; lengthen your cords, and strengthen your stakes. For you shall expand to the right and to the left." (Isaiah 54:2)

Change your thinking. **Think BIG**. *"But new wine must be put into new bottles; and both are preserved."* (Luke 5:38) **Think PAST the limits of your mind.** Stretch out your horizon of ENDEAVORS and THOUGHTS. **Color outside the lines.** *"These things began Jesus both to DO and to TEACH."* Base your thoughts, your goals, and your endeavors upon God's Holy Word. **Use your faith!**

- Spend time MEDITATING God's Word so you can LEARN His principles.

- Spend time PRAYING so you can talk to Him and HEAR from Him.

- Spend time PLANNING so you will know what to IMPLEMENT for Him.

- Spend time BELIEVING so you will know what to RECEIVE from Him.

Faith is wonderful—but it's even better when you have a PLAN to go along with your faith! If YOUR PLANS fit into the PLANS OF GOD, you will have the faith of God—and the faith of God ALWAYS WORKS!

One time I took four of my oldest children on a hike. We had looked out our window for many months across a valley and to the beautiful hills where we lived. I kept telling them that sometime we would hike up to the hills. One Saturday I surprised them and said, *"Today is the day we will hike up into the hills."* We packed a little lunch and set out upon our way. They were excited and I was, too.

As we reached the base of the hills we came across something we had never seen from our window. It was a deep stream, which was an obstacle to our forward progress. **I carried my children one by one over the ditch**. As we reached the top of the hills we saw a view of splendor. It was a beautiful lake nestled in the top of the hills that we had never seen and did not know was there.

You will never experience the majestic NEW unseen vistas in life until you're willing to venture out. **Leave the comfort zone behind and go into the Promised Land!** If you reach obstacles—*which you will*—your Father will carry you through. He will honor your FAITH. Just trust Him.

COMMON SENSE FOR CRISIS SITUATIONS

Do not be afraid of doing the wrong **right** thing! Listen to God and make a decision!

What stirs you? What makes you come to life?

Do not limit yourself by your own thoughts!

God is NOT old. He is eternally young ... AND ... He is NOT limited by **your** past disobedience.

Are YOU perishing spiritually where you are?

Is your soul lean ... or do you want to be more creative and productive?

That is, is your life not as productive as YOU and God want it to be? **Do you want BIG things to happen in your life?**

Has that dream vision you have been carrying in your heart faded and left YOU with a lean soul? Are YOU in a dry land spiritually?

If so, this is THE chapter for YOU: *Common Sense for Crisis Situations*.

Do not be afraid of doing the wrong **right** thing! Listen to God and make a decision!

This message is being written to you whether you are 5 years of age or 105. When I was a little boy, about 10 years of age, I prophesied that men would travel to the moon. No one ever dreamed—or talked about—such a thing happening. I also prophesied that I would be a minister when I grew up. The latter was probably more of a long shot statistically than the former (at least to those who knew me).

Many years later both prophecies came to pass. Think **BIG** and prophesy **BIG** when you **know** it is God.

What stirs you? What makes you come to life? When you take time to think creatively while reading God's Word, things will begin to click in your life. God will provide for you and you will be productive.

Change your thinking!

Do not limit yourself by your own thoughts!

- THINK BIG

- BELIEVE

- RECEIVE

- ACT

- MULTIPLY

- COMMISSION

Remember the acronym: **T**rue **B**lood **R**an **A**t **M**ount **C**alvary.

God is NOT old; He is eternally young.

God is NOT limited by your disobedience.

In 2 Kings Chapter 7 we see the productivity and success of anointed common sense in a time of crisis. There was a famine in the land. Also, the Syrian army laid siege to the Israelites in this area. Four (4) lepers were outside the city gates. **They were facing death because of famine**, just like the other people. But **they were also vexed with an incurable disease: leprosy**. The king and other people would not allow them to come into the city.

On a certain day the four lepers said to one another, *"Why are we sitting here until we die? If we say, 'We will enter the city,' the famine is in the city, and we shall die there. And if we sit here, we die also. Now therefore, come, let us surrender to the army of the Syrians. If they keep us alive, we shall live; and if they kill us, we shall only die."*

It is obvious that they had three (3) options with four (4) possible results:

235

- Go into the city and **die**: of famine—or, die because they were lepers and were not allowed inside.

- Stay where they were ... outside the city and **die**: of famine—or, die because the Syrians would kill them when overtaking the city.

- Get up, and go to the camp of the Syrians where there was food, AND either **die or live**: depending upon how the Syrians would treat them.

It's obvious that **the third option was the common sense option**.

God's people need an anointing of common sense. Too many times we are waiting upon a "spiritual answer" to a "common sense" alternative. The third option—the common sense option—is just what the four lepers chose to do.

When the lepers came to the outskirts of the Syrian camp, to their surprise no one was there. For the LORD had caused the army of the Syrians to hear the noise of chariots and the noise of horses—the noise of a great army; so they (the Syrians) said to one another, *"Look, the king of Israel has hired against us the kings of the Hittites and the kings of the Egyptians to attack us."*

Therefore, the Syrians arose at twilight and fled; they left everything in their camp intact: food, silver, gold, clothing, tents, horses, and donkeys. They even threw away their weapons as they fled. (2 Kings 7:3-7)

And when these lepers came to the outskirts of the camp, they went into one tent and ate and drank, and carried from it silver and gold and clothing, and went and hid *them;* then they came back and entered another tent, and carried *some* from there *also,* and went and hid *it.*

Then they said to one another, *"We are not doing right. This day is a day of good news, and we remain silent. If we wait until morning light, some punishment will come upon us. Now therefore, come, let us go and tell the king's household."*

So they went and called to the gatekeepers of the city, and told them, saying, *"We went to the Syrian camp, and surprisingly no one was there, not a human sound—only horses and donkeys tied, and the tents intact."* And the gatekeepers called out, and they told *it* to the king's household inside. (2 Kings 7:8-11)

In 24 hours the economy changed—literally overnight. It had been prophesied by Elisha the day before (2 Kings 7:1). God found four lepers who had **spiritual common sense**.

As soon as the lepers made a **MOVE**, God caused the Syrians to hear the sound of a great army.

NOTICE

When the lepers made a **MOVE**, God caused the Syrians to hear the sound of a great army.

THERE ARE THINGS IN YOUR LIFE THAT WILL NEVER HAPPEN UNTIL **YOU** USE **SPIRITUAL COMMON SENSE** AND **MOVE IN FAITH.**

If you are dying spiritually where you are at—*if you are NOT being productive*—then **use spiritual common sense** and **make the MOVE** after you have heard from God.

You may be in a situation now very similar to that of the four lepers.

You are perishing spiritually where you are. That is, your life is not as productive as God wants it to be. You want BIG things to happen in your life: to reach the world for Messiah Jesus. That dream vision you have been carrying in your heart as faded and your soul is lean. You are in a dry land spiritually.

Take a step of faith—make the move about which God is speaking to you. What do you have to lose?

238

Read the Word of God and LISTEN. Talk to Him and LISTEN. Pray in tongues and LISTEN. **Then do what He tells you to do.**

Jesus said, *"The field is the world."* (Matthew 13:38-43) Jesus also taught that if YOU want to get the treasure out of the field, you have to buy the WHOLE FIELD. (Matthew 13:44) If you want to reach China, then you have to purchase the whole field. If you want to reach Iran, then you have to purchase the whole field. **Meditate on this!**

Nothing happened until the four lepers took **THE MOVE** in the right direction.

Nothing happened until the children of Israel took **THE MOVE** and put their feet in the Red Sea.

Nothing happened until the priests of Israel took **THE MOVE** and put their feet in the River Jordan.

When you take **THE MOVE** of obedient faith ... **THEN** ... the God of Israel will cause things to happen. **He will make a way for you!** *He will cause the enemy to hear a sound of war!* Why should God do the MIRACLE if YOU are NOT going to move in faith? **He is waiting on YOU.**

Do not be afraid of doing the wrong **right** thing!

The destiny of nations and people groups is hanging in the balance.

God honors faith—that is His language.

Lay your left hand on your head and lay your right hand upon your heart and repeat these three (3) words:

NATIONS ... NATIONS ... NATIONS.

ROOF OF SILENCE AND SCIENTOLOGY

In this chapter you will learn what happened when Prince Handley went to help a Scientology Volunteer Minister ... and what came out of the Scientology worker's mouth when demons spoke through him.

You will also learn how some of God's people are actually "paralleling" *without realizing* the Scientology precepts of:

■ Release of inhibitions; and,

■ Knowledge reports.

This section will protect you from vicious cults like Scientology and, also, help you to be more empowered by God's love.

So many times we hear psychologists, and others, say that it is not good to keep things pent up inside us; that is, we **need** to express our opinions or views. They teach that we are to express ourselves outwardly and openly.

As a young minister preaching in the open air in large metropolitan cities in different countries, I would sometimes cross paths with people bound by Satan who were involved in the dangerous cult of Scientology.

They would have their disciples go out into public places and do and say foolish things to **release**—"purge" or "clear" them—of inner regressions.

One day I went—at the request of friends—to visit a Scientology Volunteer Minister, a relative of theirs about whom they were concerned. I told him that he was a "minister of Satan" and that I was a minister of Christ and had the POWER to cast the demons out of him.

A voice speaking from the Scientology worker immediately said, *"We will not come out. This is our house."* NOTICE: The use by the demon(s) speaking, using the words "**We**" and "**our**" and "**house**." (There were many demons in him.) The Scientology Minister did NOT want help and refused my offer to pray for his deliverance. **Two weeks later he was admitted to an insane asylum** and I think later committed suicide.

RELATIONSHIP OF GOSSIP & RELEASE
BOTH ARE DEMON INSPIRED

Many of God's People are doing a "release" of inner regressions—like the Scientologists—**but on a different plane: they "release" gossip** about a person by bringing up things (true, false, or imagined) about a person's past. Such people are (many times unknowingly) trying to "purge" themselves of inner hatred, bitterness or jealousy.

If we have something "inside us" that we should share with someone **privately**, we should make every effort—in love—to disclose **that to the person involved**. However, there are times when it is better, as my mother used to say, to "let sleeping dogs lie." I say it this way, *"Be quiet and pray in tongues (the language of the Holy Spirit). Then, do what God tells you to do."*

A "gossip"—a person who gossips—is defined as "**a person who likes talking about other people's private lives in a chiefly derogatory manner**." NOTE: This does NOT include a person who relays objective material for the true sake of protecting other people. (Such as a valid "whistleblower.")

We discussed in a previous chapter that the word "devil" is from the Greek "diabolos" and means "**a traducer: one who attacks the reputation of another by slander or libel**," and is synonymous with "backbiter, slanderer, defamer."

The Holy Bible also talks about **"busybodies," which in the original Greek means "to meddle, to work all around"** and **sometimes refers to the "curious arts" or the "works of Satan."** The devil is actually the source of gossip, whether true or false, and merely uses—or works through—the "instrument: the person

243

doing the gossip." **Scientologists are encouraged to "write up" fellow members**—even relatives and spouses—through the use of "Knowledge Reports."

SCIENTOLOGISTS ARE ENCOURAGED TO WRITE UP FELLOW MEMBERS THRU THE USE OF "KNOWLEDGE REPORTS"

Especially egregious is the action of a Christian, one who claims to know Christ, **who talks about another person in a defaming way**, **working around as a busybody—a gossip—about other people's private lives**. So repugnant is this action to the Lord that the Holy Spirit equates it to being a "murderer or a thief or an evildoer." *"But let none of you suffer as a murderer, or a thief, or as an evildoer, or as a busybody in other men's matters."* (1 Peter 4:15)

The Holy Bible tells us that *"Love bears all things, hopes all things, endures all things."* (Brit Chadashah: 1 Corinthians 13:7) The Greek word for **"bear"** here used is the word **"stego"** and means **"to roof over;"** that is, **"to cover with silence."** It also has the thought of "enduring patiently."

A LIE CAN TRAVEL HALFWAY AROUND THE WORLD WHILE THE TRUTH IS PUTTING ON ITS SHOES
– Mark Twain

‗‗‗‗‗‗‗‗‗‗

Love covers and conceals the faults of another person. The scripture admonishes us to *"be earnest in your love among yourselves, for LOVE covers a multitude of sins."* (1 Peter 4:8)

We need to "roof over" the sins, faults, and imperfections of others. So many of God's People are sick, incapacitated—or at the least physically not at their best—because they dig into the lives of others. They forget that God does NOT even do this, nor does He allow Satan to do this. Especially **when one gossips—*or brings forth information in a demeaning manner*—about the past of a believer in Messiah Jesus, they are going beyond the BLOOD of Christ.**

In this way they are violating the **Law of the New Creation**, and setting themselves up as little gods, declaring the BLOOD of Messiah as impotent, and NOT efficacious. *"Therefore if anyone is in Messiah, he is a new creation. The old things have passed away. Behold,* *all things have become new."* (Brit Chadashah: 2 Corinthians 5:17)

Such people receive bad reports from another, and do not even pay the person against whom the report was made the courtesy of asking them "Is this true" ... or asking ... "What is your side of the story?"

I usually tell people, *"I wasn't there, I didn't see it ... so don't tell me about it."* **A person who is empowered by God's love never makes the sins or failures of another person the subject of either censure or conversation."**

Isn't it really much easier—and better—to bring up the GOOD things about a person—past or present—than the bad? It is actually a litmus test of WHAT is inside YOU. **Look for and proclaim the GOOD—"roof over"—and cover the bad.**

Only when **current** error or danger proceeding from a person's life needs to be exposed should we consider taking the roof off of the matter. And remember: *"Judge fruit ... NOT motives."*

When you judge others, you are really taking the cover off of yourself and showing what is inside YOU. You are effectively saying, *"If I were in their shoes, I would be doing that."* *"Judge not, that you be not judged."* (Brit Chadashah: Mattiyahu / Matthew 7:1)

Love covers and conceals—it "roofs over"— everything as far as it can. If a person empowered by God's love is the only one who has knowledge of the situation, he keeps it in his own heart: **He or she "roofs over" the incident**.

I trust this teaching has helped you, my friend, and that it will help you to be more empowered by God's love.

DEALING WITH TENSION: PLUS HEALING RELATIONSHIPS

In this chapter you will learn the different types of mentalities.

Because there are problems in interpersonal relationships does NOT always mean you are sinning; for example, problems with family members.

This section will teach you different processes for dealing with tension in relationships—and for solving problems.

You will learn the BENEFIT of confrontation (which is an alternative to unacceptable behavior).

Plus—as a BONUS—you will learn HOW to separate yourself from strife so that you can appropriate God's healing and MIRACLES.

Because there are problems in interpersonal relationships does NOT mean you are sinning.

Tension in relationships is NOT bad. It is a "way mark" if handled correctly. That is, it is a marker along the way to further progress, an ensign for the strengthening of the relationship.

There are four (4) types of mentalities:

- Survival

- Contract

- Traditional (family)

- Covenant

In the covenant relationship, you are being concerned MORE for the other party. Dr. Livingstone, the great missionary to Africa, reached many tribes for Christ that could not have been reached otherwise by making a blood covenant with them.

In such covenant relationships each party is telling the other: *"Whatever I have is yours if you need it."* Livingstone had a life threatening condition that required him to drink goats' milk. Because of this, he would keep a goat with him. One day, a tribal chieftain that had made a blood covenant with Livingstone told him that he wanted his white goat. That reminds me of the saying *"Got your goat!"* Knowing the seriousness of this request, and the danger it could pose for himself, Livingstone honored the request and gave the chieftain his white goat.

Many of our problems appear in our relationships with other people. Has anyone ever had problems with you?

Moses was a problem solver; he was an intercessor. You can read about his intercession and leadership through using prayer in Numbers Chapter 14. **The FIRST thing to do when tension arises in a relationship is to PRAY**.

Because there are problems in interpersonal relationships doesn't mean you are sinning; for example, problems with family members. If you are praying for the other person or people—*if you are forgiving*—and if you are doing what the Holy Spirit is showing you to do (which never contradicts Scripture), then be at peace. However, **many people—and even some Christians—"stumble" in life because they are proceeding in darkness**. Some Christians even experience lots of sickness and repeated physical conditions ... *or even accidents* ... because of this.

Our beloved brother John admonishes us in his writings as follows:

> *"He who says he is in the light, and hates his brother, is in darkness until now.*
>
> *He who loves his brother abides in the light, and there is no cause for stumbling in him.*
>
> *But he who hates his brother is in darkness and walks in darkness, and does not know where he*

is going, because the darkness has blinded his eyes." (1 John 2:9-11)

This is also why it is important NOT to cause trouble in a relationship between other people. The Bible says that **one of the seven things that are an abomination to God—and that he hates—is the person "who causes discord among brethren."** (Proverbs 6:19)

CAUTION: If a person who is NOT in either a traditional (family blood) relationship with you or a covenant relationship with you, comes to you and says something negatively about—*or brings charges against*—a person in your family or with whom you are in relationship, BEWARE! **Many families and relationships have been injured by such people**. Your first reaction OR response should be as follows: *"I will consult with my relative or partner about this (what you have told me) and then I will pray and take it to the Lord."*

Many people have received lies about their own family members or partners while never having even asked about "**the other side of the story**," or WHY the accusations have been made—or even IF they were true. My mother used to say, "Blood is thicker than water."

Moses led 3,000,000 people. In Numbers Chapter 14, Moses had just finished asking—interceding—for God's mercy on Israel when Korah, Dathan, and Abiram started their rebellion against him. Korah was Moses' cousin and a member of the tribe of Levi in the family of Aaron. (Numbers 16:3)

Notice five (5) processes in the life of Moses in dealing with tension in relationships and solving problems:

- Personal Prayer

- Confrontation

- Let God Fight for You

- Separate Yourself from Strife

- Intercede for Others

PERSONAL PRAYER

In Numbers 16:4-7 notice that Moses positioned himself face down in prayer. First, always PRAY and SEEK GOD'S WISDOM. Are you facing a problem? Are you causing a problem?

Korah's complaint against Aaron was strictly a complaint against God: it was not a complaint about qualifications, but against God's order. This can often be a cause of spiritual impotence—and of judgment—among churches, ministries, or families.

In 1 Corinthians 11: 3 we see God's order for the home: *"But I want you to know that the head of every man is*

Christ, the head of the woman is man, and the head of Christ is God."

It is NOT a matter of who is better than another, but rather of order, so that love and power can flow unhindered from God: to effect BLESSING upon the unit and upon the individuals of the unit. In cases where an individual is NOT performing their duties ... for example, when a man is not being the spiritual leader of the home, then God has ways to circumvent the hindrance so that blessing will flow. This is where prayer and obedience come into play by each member. PRAY, LISTEN, and OBEY!

CONFRONTATION

Dathan and Abiram were members of the tribe of Reuben, while Moses was of the tribe of Levi. It was important for Moses to control his anger. **We are to approach people in God's wisdom and love so they will receive BENEFIT of confrontation** (which is an alternative to unacceptable behavior).

■ Pray for God's wisdom; and,

■ Follow up with appropriate confrontation.

Let people know, if it is possible, that you are confronting them because you love them and want the best for them.

As parents, God tells us to correct without anger. We may have to spank (use the rod, not the hand) at times, but we should always, after the discipline, pray with our children and let them KNOW they are FORGIVEN and LOVED.

God did NOT invent "time out." "Time out" has probably done more to make it hard for young people to honor, hear from, and serve God than any other socially devised concept during the ages. It is probably one of the major factors for the increased number of teen pregnancies.

> *"And you, fathers, do not provoke your children to wrath, but bring them up in the training and admonition of the LORD."* (Ephesians 6:4)

LET GOD FIGHT FOR YOU

After you have first prayed and done what God has showed you to do ... then REST! We see two good examples of this in Exodus Chapter 14 and 2 Chronicles Chapter 20.

"Stand still, and see the salvation of the LORD, which He will accomplish for you today ... the LORD will fight for you, and you shall hold your peace." (Exodus 13-14)

"Do not be afraid nor dismayed because of this great multitude, for the battle is not yours, but God's." (2 Chronicles 20:15)

We also **see what happened** to those who rebelled against Moses and Aaron in Numbers 16:28-30.

Has God ever lost a battle? **NO!** Have you? YES!

SEPARATE YOURSELF FROM STRIFE

When you need deliverance, separate yourself from struggle ... and let God do a MIRACLE!

MENTALLY SEPARATE YOURSELF

If you are thinking negative thoughts, separate yourself from these and renew your mind with the promises in God's Word.

PHYSICALLY SEPARATE YOURSELF

You may have to separate yourself from either a SITUATION or a PERSON. In Exodus Chapter Two we read where Moses killed a man. He then spent 40 years in the wilderness of Midian, probably in the eastern part of the Sinai Peninsula or northwestern Arabia. I, personally, have walked alone with 19 camels in that Sinai desert. There, under the tutelage of God, Moses learned how to control himself ... and how to control a flock. After that, he became Israel's pastor for 40 years.

Think about YOUR lifestyle. You may have to separate yourself from ungodly relationships or counter productive relationships.

INTERCEDE FOR OTHERS

Six times Moses interceded for the lives of Israel. On one occasion, God told Moses that he would even wipe out the complaining Israelites and give Moses a NEW nation, greater and mightier than they, to start over. However, Moses interceded for the people and talked God into sparing them. (Numbers 14:11-24)

After the incident where God judged Korah, Dathan, and Abiram, the children of Israel went immediately back to complaining, and accused Moses of killing them. Because of this, another 14,700 people died. (Numbers 16:41)

Notice, "the children of Korah died not." (Numbers 26:11) Years later, we read about the children (descendants) of Korah being ministers in the tabernacle (1 Chronicles 9:19). They also wrote many Psalms. God had warned the people to depart from the rebels and get away from their tents before judgment fell. **Evidently, someone in Korah's family made a quality decision.**

There is a truth here: **You may have to walk away from a relationship—or a relative—at some time in your life. But only do it after MUCH PRAYER**, seeking

God's will and not yours; and KNOWING it is what God wants at that time! It doesn't mean that you don't love them, or that you're not willing to help them. Read Genesis Chapter 13 and Mark 10:29.

Above all, never forget what Jesus promised you, *"I will never leave you nor forsake you."* (Hebrews 13:5) And ... always forgive!

Forgiveness can save most relationships. God is our perfect model. In the Book of Hosea, God pictures Israel as a harlot gone away from her husband. After all the times Israel disobeyed God, as a disobedient wife, He still promises her a glorious future:

> *"I will betroth you to me forever; Yes I will betroth you to Me in righteousness and justice, in loving kindness and mercy; I will betroth you to me in faithfulness, and you shall know the LORD."*

> – Hosea 2:19-20

HOW TO RECOVER LOSS ... TAKE IT BACK

Many times loss is the result of a particular **stratagem of Satan to get you to STOP action**, or to DISCOURAGE you from going forward.

There can be as many types of loss as there are activities or relationships in which we are involved. This chapter will teach you **HOW to recover loss**.

Hard times are many times a sign that **you are entering a NEW dimension of service to God ... and blessing**: for YOU and for the people you will be serving.

In the future economic chaos that will encompass the world you may—if NOT prepared—suffer financial and material loss.

This section will help you to recover all ... and to do greater works for the LORD.

Many times, hard or difficult times are a good sign, especially for the People of God.

If you have lived long enough, it is quite possible you have encountered some type of loss ... or let me put it this way: **suffered some kind of loss.** "Suffered" because any type of loss can cause you some kind of mental or physical anguish. What you want to be aware of—and guard against—is that you **do not allow the loss to cause "anguish of the spirit."**

Many times loss is the result of a particular **stratagem of Satan to get you to STOP action**, or to DISCOURAGE you from going forward, or to harass you mentally and CONFUSE you so you do not focus on the important goals of the Kingdom of God: especially the ordained purpose of your existence at this particular time of your life.

At times, the loss we encounter **may be our own fault** as the result of:

- Ignorance (lack of knowledge in a specific area);

- Disobedience to God's Law;

- Not taking advantage of information available to us;

- Presumption; and,

- Foolishness (like gambling).

There can be as many types of loss as there are activities or relationships in which we are involved.

- Financial loss;

- Loss of a loved one;

- Physical or mental loss due to health issues;

- Loss of the anointing of the Holy Spirit.

In this chapter I want to teach you **HOW to recover loss.** (I was on my way to ride my motorcycle all day when God instructed me STOP and to give this word—this message—to His people.)

Many times, hard or difficult times are a good sign, especially for the People of God.

For example, a physical condition or material situation—or just **tough things—will crop up right before you are entering a NEW dimension of service to God**.

You might not be aware that a NEW dimension of service to the LORD is about to unfold ... OR ... you may have been praying and fasting for it.

A NEW level or area of service to God is extremely important for the people you will be reaching—AND—for the Lord you are serving: Jesus the Messiah.

In First Samuel Chapter 30, we read that when King David and his men returned to Ziklag they discovered their wives and children and all their property had been taken by the Amalekites.

When consulting with the LORD, David was directed to *"Pursue, for you shall surely overtake them, and without fail recover all."*

The message for you is to *"Go, recover all the enemy has stolen from you."* **Bind Satan in JESUS' name and command him to repay you seven times for everything he has stolen from you.** *"Men do not despise a thief, if he steal to satisfy his soul when he is hungry; but if he be found, **he shall restore sevenfold**; he shall give all the substance of his house."* (Proverbs 6:30-31)

How much more shall the devil—using either people OR his demonic agents to steal from you—**be commanded in JESUS' name to restore to you sevenfold, if not more!**

Notice that David and his men not only recovered their wives, children, and property that had been stolen ... but, also, recovered all the spoil the Amalekites had stolen from the Philistines and out of the land of Judah.

Notice, also, that right before this happened, **David was greatly distressed** (when his men discovered their loss) because **the people were considering stoning him**. However, *"David encouraged himself in the LORD his God."* (1 Samuel 30:6)

A few days later after recovering the losses at Ziklag, **plus extra riches**, David received word that his enemy,

King Saul, had been slain in battle. David then went up to Hebron, where the men of Judah anointed him King over Judah. (Even though the LORD's Prophet Samuel had anointed him King previously.)

SUMMARY

Hard times are many times a sign that **you are entering a NEW dimension of service to God … and blessing**: for YOU and for the people you will be serving.

Hard times are many times a sign that **the devil is greatly concerned about the NEW dimension of service you will be entering, and** therefore **is trying to defeat you through discouragement so that you will roll over and quit.** Do NOT do it. **Get up, ACT, and recover it all**.

In hard times you have **an EXCELLENT opportunity to encourage** others:

- They can see your trust in God.

- Your declaration of faith will position you into God's favor.

- Your testimony will encourage others to KNOW or GROW Messiah Jesus in their lives.

SUGGESTION

Get alone with God and and LISTEN to Him. (You may want to fast.)

If your loss has been financial or material—*like many people will experience in future economic chaos*—then make a COVENANT with God.

Tell Him that you want to give him a certain amount **above** your normal tithes and offerings for a certain amount of time OR a certain length of new venture you are entering. (See Tanakh: Malachi Chapter Three, verses 10-11.) You can give this money to your Synagogue or Church or Prayer Group ... or to the needy or orphans or widows.

Learn to work with God "hand-in-hand" to bless the nations. This is TRUE prosperity.

"But you shall remember the LORD your God: **for it is He that gives you power to get wealth**, *so that he may establish his covenant which he swore unto your fathers ..."* (Torah: Deuteronomy 8:18)

Remember: the devil wants to kill you, steal from you and destroy you. But the GOOD NEWS is that God's Son—Messiah Yeshua—came to Planet Earth that YOU might have life ... and have it MORE ABUNDANTLY. This is God's will for you—in addition to eternal life in Heaven!

Get up, ACT, and recover it all!

A MAJOR SECRET FOR HEALTH

One of the greatest means of healing today is simply by means of REST. You heard right: **rest!**

First of all, healing through rest is a promise provided for us in the Holy Bible. In the Tanakh, we read:

> "*If you keep your feet from stomping on the Sabbath—from pursuing your own interests on my holy day—if you call the Sabbath a delight and the Lord's Holy Day honorable; and if you honor it by not going your own ways and seeking your own pleasure or speaking merely idle words, then you will take delight in the Lord, and he will make you ride upon the high places of the earth; and he will make you feast on the inheritance of your ancestor Jacob, your father. Yes! The mouth of the Lord has spoken.*" – Isaish 58:13-14

Notice, when you "**ride on the heights of the earth**" you have dominion ... you have perspective and are ABOVE the things of the earth. You are in a position of blessing by God. **You are blessed**. Also, when you "**feast on the inheritance of you ancestor Jacob**" you are partaking spiritually—plus physically and materially—of the health and wealth of the father of the 12 tribes of Israel.

Notice something interesting. In the context of Isaiah Chapter 58 we read about fasting as well as rest. In my personal experience, one of the quickest ways to receive healing is through "fasting unto the **LORD.**" Sometimes, just a three day fast with water only—or, even a three day fast until 7 PM (and then eating healthy food)—has brought immediate healing. Notice what God promises in Isaiah Chapter 58 concerning fasting: *"Then your light will break forth like the dawn, and **your healing will spring up quickly**; and your vindication will go before you, and the glory of the Lord will guard your back. Then you'll call, and the Lord will answer; you'll cry for help, and He will respond, 'I am here.'"* – Verses 8 and 9

Let me give you a personal testimony of how God used REST to bring me healing. I had been very busy holding evangelistic and tent meetings and in addition I had contracted for a busy schedule of radio production. Quickly I was entered into the Intensive Care center of the hospital with **several unknown rare diseases**. I was placed into an isolation room where even **the nurse was NOT allowed to enter**.

When the nurse was taking my information (she had to stand outside the door), she asked me, *"What is your date of birth."* I asked her, *"Which one do you want?"* She said, *"Do you mean that you have been born more than once?"* I said, *"Yes, when I came out of my mother's womb … AND … when I gave my life to Jesus Christ."* She answered, *"I know what you're talking about. My father is a minister; but **I have never experienced the new birth**."* (I don't remember if she received the **LORD** there or not.) Then she asked me, *"What is your address?"* I then told her, *"Heaven."*

The nurse came back in a vew minutes and said, *"Where were you? The doctor came in to see you in your room and you were NOT there."* I said, *"I have NOT left."* Then I realized that I was on the other side of my bed on the ground praying and the doctor could not see me from where he stood at the door.

Anyway, as soon as I was placed in the isolation ward room, I placed my hands behind my head ... and laying back ... **I realized instantly WHY I was there.** In a moment, the LORD impressed on my mind the verse from Isaiah 30:15: *"In returning and **rest** you shall be saved; in quietness and in confidence shall be your strength: **and you would not."***

I then realized I had been busy doing God's work holding tent and evangelistic meetings, working to support the ministry, and travelling ... but NOT taking my Day of Rest. When I realized this, I repented before the **LORD** and asked for His forgiveness. Instantly, I could tell that I had been healed.

My friend, truly God has given YOU a practical and effective—cost effective—means of healing: REST.

> *"Take my yoke upon you, and learn of me; for I am meek and lowly in heart: and you shall find **rest** unto your souls."* – Jesus of Nazareth

*"In returning and **rest** you shall be saved; in quietness and in confidence shall be your strength."* – Isaiah 30:15

If you want to meet the Healer—*Jesus the Anointed One*—NOW is the time! Invite God's Son, Jesus, to come into your life by praying the following prayer:

"Messiah Jesus, I know that you are The Great Physician. You loved me enough to shed your sinless blood and die for me on the cross stake that I might be healed. I know you are alive. Please forgive my sins, come into my life, and be my Master. Help me to live for you, and take me to Heaven when I die."

PREPARE AHEAD OF TIME FOR THREATS

I presented the material in this chapter several years ago ... but NOW the threat is more imminent.

As you study the details of what would happen as a result of EMP attacks, you will be aware of:

■ What to **PRAY** for ahead of time; and,

■ What to **PREPARE** for ahead of time.

This is NO idle threat. Recently Ted Koppel (American broadcast journalist), and past news anchor for *Nightline*, wrote the book *Lights Out*, in which he described what would happen IF and WHEN electric power grids are/were attacked by either cyber attack or EMP attack.

I believe that my report better describes—and with simplistic detail—the scenario of what the results of such attack would be where the "rubber hits the road."

Israel and the USA are targets of EMP weapons attack. Either country, Israel or the US, would be brought to—for all practical near term purposes—an irreversible standstill. EMP attacks could be delivered to Israel from a freighter by missile or an Iranian missile off the coasts of either country ... or from beer cans without an air attack.

Israel and the USA are targets of EMP weapons attack. EMP—Electro Magnetic Pulse—occurs when a nuclear device is detonated (either from aircraft or missiles ... or from **a terrorist device as small as a beer can**).

The most potentially damaging would be from a high altitude nuclear explosion. Both Israel and the USA are militarily on ultra high technical systems. **An EMP device would disengage sophisticated electrical gear like sensors, power grids, and computers.**

EMP attacks could be delivered to Israel **from a freighter** by missile **off the Mediterranean coast** (or, to the USA off the Pacific (West), Atlantic (East), Gulf of Mexico (South), or Great Lakes (North).

Dr. Fred Levien, retired US Navy Commander and government consultant, states that **on a 1 to 10 scale, the threat is a number 8**.

An EMP attack would also result in:

- Refrigerators not working;

- Dead livestock;

- Decomposition of food;

- Factories closed;

- Military standstill;

- Communications stop; and,

269

■ Businesses fail.

The Mossad and the CIA know this. The IDF and AMAN and US Armed Forces and Pentagon know this. **They do NOT want you and the general public to know this as it will bring alarm. However, I want you to know so you will know WHAT to do**: for your protection, your family protection, your business and economic protection ... and the nation of Israel's protection

HOW EMP WORKS

An EMP nuclear detonation produces an **electromagnetic** field with a super fast transient **pulse** which couples itself to power lines, cables, antennas, and sends an electric surge (or, spike). It literally **fries the electronic system in a vehicle**, resulting in NO ignition. Lights and windows will work because of the battery, but the auto will NOT run.

Terrorists could wipe out Ben Gurion Airport, or Kennedy Airport, plus a host of other targets. **Air Traffic Control would become disabled**. There would be no communications. **Planes in the sky would be left flying blind and many would crash after running out of fuel**.

EMP DEVICES THE SIZE OF BEER CANS – NO NEED FOR AIR ATTACKS

Terrorists could target financial centers. For example, the NYSE (New York stock Exchange) could be wiped out with individuals and companies **losing billions of dollars**.

An air attack on either Israel or the US could take months ...or even years ... from which to recover.

However, **a hand EMP device (the size of a beer can) could be used at airports, financial or communications centers, hospitals, power companies, police or military bases, and urban traffic and transit control centers ... not only by rogue nations, but by terrorist groups such as ISIS ... and by deranged psychotic individuals**.

Militarily, EMP weapons can disable vehicles, even heavy armored vehicles, in a single hit. **Data transfers are also jammed, resulting in NO communications: medical, military, financial, personal, power, water, lights, sanitation**.

Either country, Israel or the US, would be brought to, for all practical near term purposes, an irreversible standstill.

THE RESULTS OF EMP ATTACK

The first 24 hours would be absolute chaos!

An EMP attack **would reach apogee in a matter of minutes**. It would **destroy GPS, telecommunications, water delivery, and power grids**. The greatest damage would be from a nuclear detonated device 40 to 400 KM

(25 to 250 miles) above land. An air attack could wipe out all of the USA (and the North American continent). **However, it could be fired from freighter by a Scud or missile off coastal waters**. Such a coastal attack from a freighter in the Mediterranean could easily shut down all of Israel.

A terrorist EMP attack might profoundly affect any major city; however, because of the high cost of real estate and traffic issues, **some** major businesses have relocated valuable assets outside of major urban areas, and have taken other measures to protect themselves. Therefore, the long-term economic and technological impact of such an event might not be as grave as previously imagined, depending on the nature of the original attack.

A common scenario is detonation of a device using long-range missiles available only to major military powers. The greater the altitude, the greater the destruction. An EMP device fired from 30 miles altitude in the US Midwest would shut down six (6) or seven (7) states. However, **an offshore detonation at high altitude would disrupt both an entire coast and regions hundreds of miles inland** (e.g. 120 mile altitude, 1000 mile EMP radius). Moreover, a high altitude burst could be positioned over international waters **by means of a missile of low accuracy**, launched from a ship, also in international waters. North Korea, Iran, and Pakistan (for example) have Scud-derived missiles of more than adequate capability. **Likewise, the Iranian SHAHAB missile**.

Such an attack on either Israel or the USA would take either country (even though Israel attained statehood in 1948) back to the 1800's as far as technology is concerned.

ELECTRIC POWER GRIDS

This is NO idle threat. Recently Ted Koppel (American broadcast journalist), and past news anchor for *Nightline*, wrote the book *Lights Out*, in which he described what would happen IF and WHEN electric power grids are/were attacked by either cyber attack or EMP attack.

The USA electric system is in serious danger of widespread blackouts that could last months as a result of destruction of sensitive, hard to replace, equipment, At the current time, government agencies have no reliable statistics dealing with sub-station attacks.

WARNING

THE USA ELECTRIC SYSTEM IS IN DANGER OF WIDESPREAD, PROLONGED BLACKOUTS.

The Federal Energy Regulatory Commission regulates the interstate power system requires utilities to protect substations that could cause blackouts in the power grid network if attacked. However, this requirement does NOT extend to the tens of thousands of smaller substations.

If multiple (8 to 10, for example) substations were attacked at once, it could take months to recover ... to get power back in operation ... even with generators as backup. Think of the effect on hospitals, cooking, sanitation, transportation, communications and life!

Many of the KEY generators are outdated, made overseas, and way too large to be transported practically once INSIDE the USA by rail or road. Plus, manufacture will take months. This is the weakest link in the USA grid.

Nuclear attack(s) by evil empires such as Iran (which may NOT be successful against the USA) will be replaced by tactical cyber warfare against the power grid. And the source of such attacks may NOT even be identifiable.

In a series titled, *Security in the North American Grid— A Nation at Risk*, George Cotter (former chief scientist at the National Security Agency) reports *"This [electric power] industry is simply unrealistic in believing in the resiliency of this Grid subject to a sophisticated attack. When such an attack occurs, make no mistake, there will be major loss of life and serious crippling of National Security capabilities."*

The reason for "breakins" at substations (and many have already happened) is to acquire information about the electric system: to get "into" the system. This can be used by terrorists at a later time. In 2011, 2.7 million utility customers lost power in Arizona, New Mexico and California due to system errors. Raw sewage flowed into the ocean. Traffic was jammed and flights were cancelled. Many substations only have a padlock on the gate with no cameras and no motion sensors or alarms

ASSESSMENT OF THE CURRENT THREAT

A report from the Federal Commission (USA) to *Assess the Threat to the United States from Electromagnetic Pulse (EMP) Attack* has painted a **bleak picture for America** under such attack: Electricity grids down, uncontrolled fires from exploding gas transport systems, no communication to summon firefighters and if they could come, no water to battle fires. All in city after city after city.

The 200-page report says Americans should **look to past incidents, then multiply those** impacts by the number of cities that could be hit by such an attack. **For example**:

San Diego County Water Authority (USA) and San Diego County Gas and Electric companies experienced severe electromagnetic interference. *Both companies found themselves unable to actuate critical valve openings and closings. This inability*

*necessitated sending technicians to remote locations to manually open and close water and gas valves, averting, in the words of a subsequent letter of complaint by the San Diego County Water Authority to the Federal Communications Commission, a **potential 'catastrophic failure' of the aqueduct system**.*

The report explained the potential impact could have included an "aqueduct rupture" with disruption of service, severe flooding and related damage to private and public property. **The source of the 1999 problem? "Errant radar on a ship 25 miles off the coast of San Diego," the report said.**

A simple problem caused a potential catastrophic failure. **Think what an EMP attack would do?!**

For more info on Nuclear, Biological and Chemical Warfare, Cyber Attacks, Radiological Warfare PLUS **Electric Grid susceptibility to attacks**, go to www.uofe.org/nbc---biowarfare.html

WHAT TO WATCH FOR

In the Tanakh, **the Prophet Daniel** (in Ketuvim), **tells us of a coming world dictator who will make a treaty (a covenant) with Israel for seven (7) years (Daniel 9:27)**. As concession for signing this treaty, **the New World Order leader will allow Israel to build her Temple on or near the Temple Mount**.

This coming world leader (the False Messiah) who will be chosen by the New Global Governance (the EU and the UN with League of Arab States) will then, **in the middle of the seven years** (after 42 months) go into the Temple and desecrate it. **He will cause the sacrifice** (zebach) **and oblation** (minchah) **to cease; he will blaspheme G-d and even claim the he** (the False Messiah) **is G-d**. This will usher in the next 42 months (the last half of the seven years) which will be **the time of greatest persecution the Jewish People have ever known** (greater than the Holocaust under Nazi Germany).

We also know that the Brit Chadashah (the New Covenant – See Mattiyahu 24:15) tells us that **Yeshua validated the prophecy of Daniel**, saying:

"When ye therefore shall see the abomination of desolation, spoken of by Daniel the prophet, stand in the holy place, (whoso reads, let him understand:)

Then let them which be in Judaea flee into the mountains:

Let him which is on the housetop not come down to take anything out of his house:

Neither let him which is in the field return back to take his clothes.

And woe unto them that are with child, and to them that give suck in those days!

But pray ye that your flight be not in the winter, neither on the Sabbath day:

For then shall be great tribulation, such as was not since the beginning of the world to this time, no, nor ever shall be.

And except those days should be shortened, there should no flesh be saved: but for the elect's sake those days shall be shortened.

Then if any man shall say unto you, Lo, here is Messiah, or there; believe it not.

For there shall arise false messiahs, and false prophets, and shall show great signs and wonders; insomuch that, if it were possible, they shall deceive the very elect.

Behold, I have told you before.

Wherefore if they shall say unto you, 'Behold, he is in the desert; go not forth: behold, he is in the secret chambers; believe it not.'

For as the lightning comes out of the east, and shines even unto the west; so shall also the coming of the Son of man be."

The False Messiah will come into office first as a peace maker. He will use the Israeli-Palestinian conflict, the Iranian-Syria-Middle East conflict, and the City of

Jerusalem as his bargaining chips. Do NOT be deceived.

Do NOT trust him. Make sure you know the REAL MESSIAH.

Pray to the God of Abraham, Isaac, and Jacob. Ask Him to reveal to you if Yeshua is really your Messiah. If He does, then receive Him and do what He asks you to do.

After you know the REAL Messiah you will be able to claim His protection: the BLOOD covering. The Torah tells in Leviticus 17:11, that the BLOOD is an atonement (kaphar), a **covering** for the soul. **Speak the BLOOD of Messiah Yeshua (Jesus) over the door of your heart: over yourself and your home by faith ...** just like the children of Israel put the BLOOD on the door of their homes that first Passover. Ask God to protect you.

LIVE A LIFE OF EXCELLENCE!

If you want to know specifically what will happen in the near future through 2030—and in the remaining days of Planet Earth—you need to study the following books in the *Prophecy Series* by Prince Handley:

Map of the End Times

Flow Chart of Revelation

Prophecy, Transition & Miracles

Babylon the Bitch: Enemy of Israel

Enhanced Humans: Mystery Matrix

Anarchy and Revolution: A Prophecy

Israel and Middle East: Past Present Future

Prophetic Calendar of Israel and the Nations

OTHER BOOKS BY PRINCE HANDLEY

LISTED ON TWO PAGES

Map of the End Times

How to Do Great Works

Flow Chart of Revelation

Action Keys for Success

Health and Healing Complete Guide to Wholeness

Prophetic Calendar for Israel & the Nations: Thru 2023

Healing Deliverance

How to Receive God's Power with Gifts of the Spirit

Healing for Mental and Physical Abuse

Victory Over Opposition and Resistance

Healing of Emotional Wounds

How to Be Healed and Live in Divine Health

Healing from Fear, Shame and Anger

How to Receive Healing and Bring Healing to Others

New Global Strategy: Enabling Missions

The Art of Christian Warfare

Success Cycles and Secrets

New Testament Bible Studies (A Study Manual)

Babylon the Bitch – Enemy of Israel

Resurrection Multiplication – Miracle Production

Faith and Quantum Physics – Your Future

Conflict Healing – Relational Health

Decision Making 101 – Know for Sure

Total Person Toolbox

Prophecy, Transition & Miracles

Enhanced Humans – Mystery Matrix

Israel and Middle East – Past Present Future

Anarchy and Revolution: A Prophecy

Real Miracles for Normal People

Sexual Immorality: Addiction of Loss

Healing Toolbox Plus: A to Z Workshop

Anointed Strategies: Power Plays

AVAILABLE AT AMAZON AND OTHER BOOK STORES

UNIVERSITY OF EXCELLENCE PRESS
San Diego ▪ London ▪ Tel Aviv

282

BONUS

To help you, and to help you teach others,
we have prepared FREE the following:

Rabbinical Studies
French Bible Studies
English Bible Studies
Spanish Bible Studies

Go to this site: www.uofe.org/biblical-studies.html

UNIVERSITY OF EXCELLENCE PRESS
San Diego ▪ London ▪ Tel Aviv

+

NOTE

For information on Prince Handley Seminars
contact: handleyworldservices@gmail.com

www.ingramcontent.com/pod-product-compliance
Lightning Source LLC
Chambersburg PA
CBHW060229050426
42448CB00009B/1360